ABOUT

Vivienne Menkes-Ivry is a Br_____rly nine years, during which she _____re. She returned to Britain in 19____ ____ ___tes for a number of British, French and American magazines. She still spends part of the year in France and has also published two books on Paris and one on Alsace.

A HANDY GUIDE TO

BUYING A HOME IN
FRANCE

VIVIENNE MENKES-IVRY

Revised Edition

SIMON & SCHUSTER

LONDON • SYDNEY • NEW YORK • TOKYO • TORONTO

First edition published in Great Britain as
Buying a House in France by
Simon & Schuster Ltd in 1990
Reprinted 1991
Second edition 1993

**Simon & Schuster Ltd, West Garden Place,
Kendal Street, London W2 2AQ**

Simon & Schuster of Australia Pty Ltd, Sydney

British Library Cataloguing-in-Publication Data
available

ISBN 0-671-712586

Design: Phil O'Sullivan
Map: Perrot Cartographics
Typesetting: Florencetype Ltd, Kewstoke, Avon
Printed in Great Britain by The Bath Press, Avon

CONTENTS

To my sister Suzy, who had the vision and sense to buy her *tas de pierres* long before it became fashionable.

INTRODUCTION
TO THE SECOND EDITION

Until the late eighties, a second home in France was a rare commodity for the British, restricted to the very rich with villas or luxury flats on the Côte d'Azur, inveterate Francophiles who long ago bought pretty houses in Provence or Burgundy, and a pioneering band who did up tumbledown farmhouses in areas off the beaten track like the Ardèche.

Although the idea of moving permanently to France had been attracting growing numbers of Britons for many years, the true invasion of second-home owners is a more recent phenomenon. Enticed by visions of ridiculously cheap barns crying out for conversion, of lazy summer days in their very own French retreat, of a quality of life that seems to be sadly lacking in modern Britain, thousands of families have boldly struck out and turned their dreams into reality. And despite the recession and the volatility of exchange rates following sterling's departure from the ERM, many more are contemplating the same step, as the Channel Tunnel and the Single European Market bring France both physically and psychologically nearer, making weekend breaks in the unspoilt countryside or on long sandy beaches a viable alternative to overcrowded British roads or endless airport delays on the way to more distant destinations.

Prices are still low in most of France compared to Britain and the recession has had the advantage, from the buyer's point of view, of weeding out the less experienced agents and other operators in the market, with the result that you are less likely to find yourself being rushed into a deal than in a boom time when it is only too easy for inexperienced or cowboy intermediaries to pressurize you into making the wrong decision. Moreover the advent of the Single European Market has simplified some procedures for citizens of other EC countries: for instance the abolition of customs controls has made moving furniture to France much easier.

This book aims to paint a realistic picture of what finding and buying a home in France involves, and explains how to select the most suitable region, who to turn to for advice and assistance – and what it will all cost.

I lived in France for many years. I hope that my own experiences, and those of the many people I have spoken to while preparing this book, will smooth your path and open your eyes to some aspects you may not have considered. But I must emphasise that no book can be a substitute for expert legal and financial advice tailored to your own circumstances, and that as laws and procedures change frequently, you must check whether the situation has altered by the time you decide to proceed.

This book is designed mainly for those thinking of buying a second home. But although I have no space to go into the financial and other implications of changing countries, I hope that it will also be a useful starting point for anyone contemplating a permanent move. Despite a number of scare stories in the British press about the British selling up *en masse* in France, the majority of home-owners remain happy with their new French abode and are managing to keep up mortgage payments. As I have pointed out in the final chapter, many of those selling up are people who moved to France permanently without proper advance planning, and found it impossible to make a living, or to earn enough to live in the style they had envisaged. And although it is written primarily from a British standpoint, I know from letters I have received from outside Britain that it has also proved useful to nationals of other countries planning to buy a home in France.

I have no space either to mention by name all the many people who kindly provided me with information for both this and the previous edition. But I am particularly grateful to Graeme Hyde and Caroline Mackie of David Marr Limited for advising on restoration costs; to Stephen Smith, running the French Department at Prettys, for keeping me constantly up to date on changing legislation and other aspects of the French property market; and to Evelyne Berthelin Ward for an invaluable Franco-British insight into the whole topic; to my sister Suzy Menkes for advice and anecdotes drawn from her many years as a second-home owner; Rosemary and Peter Farley for sharing their experiences as more recent residents and B-&-B providers; Sylvia and Andrew Martin and Carola and Peter Zentner for supplying news of their purchasing as it happened. Francis Puche of the Crédit Agricole in Cahors, Bernard Gaumont in Tours, Heather Buttery, then of Hubert Jardin, Philip and Patricia Hawkes of Philip Hawkes, Vivian Bridge of Northern France Properties, M. Dubuc in Normandy, Caroline Jenkins of Office notarial de Fréjus, Frank Rutherford of Rutherfords, Zigi Davenport of Alpine Apartments, James Daunt of Daunt Books, Ian Purslow in the Gers, M. Flahaut and John Bee in Cahors were particularly generous with their time.

Many thanks to all of them, to M. Saussard of Alain Viot and Marcel Durand, notaires associés, who ensured that my own property transactions went through smoothly, and to the other specialists, too numerous to mention by name, who supplied me with information.

V. M-I, March 1993

An asterisk (*) following the name of a company or
other organisation indicates that it is included in the list
of addresses at the end of the relevant chapter.

1 MAKING THE DECISION

Buying property is a major step, not to be taken lightly. Although prices are still generally low in France by British standards, even when the pound is weak against the franc, you are still talking about an investment of tens of thousands of pounds at the lowest, perhaps hundreds of thousands. Moreover, you are launching into a new country where things are done differently, where costs are different, where the language is different, where the people are different from what you are used to at home. Even if you speak French and visit France frequently, in buying property you will often find yourself on unfamiliar territory.

The watchword of this first chapter is: Look Before You Leap! It aims to help you to think the whole project through carefully at the outset, and save you possible anguish and expensive mistakes. And to highlight potential pitfalls that may not have occurred to you.

Making decisions in a hurry, when faced with an unexpected problem, is a recipe for disaster. I have therefore set out the key aspects to be considered, so that you can mull them over at your leisure, discuss them with your partner or family, and then take a rational, informed decision.

You may decide, when you have considered all these points, that you are not yet ready to buy a property in France. Or even that you do not want to buy in France at all. But at least you will have thought your decision through. Most probably you will go ahead, but perhaps not in the way you had originally envisaged. For instance, after weighing the question carefully, you may feel that your dream farmhouse miles from anywhere was not really what would be most suitable for you and plump for something closer to shops and other amenities.

Your decision will, of course, be subjective. I have certainly not tried to formulate any hard-and-fast rules about what you should and shouldn't decide. But I do hope that you will consider all the following points – set out as a series of questions – very carefully indeed before making up your mind. A useful French expression to know is *agir en connaissance de cause* – to act with full knowledge of the case or circumstances. My aim in this first chapter has been to ensure that this phrase fits your state of preparedness for what should be an exciting venture.

Key question 1:
Why are you thinking of buying a home in France?
This may seem an obvious question, but it affects many aspects of your final decision. The following subsidiary questions should help you answer the key question.

Do you intend it purely for your personal use or as an investment?
If it is to be for your personal use only:

3

Is it to be a holiday home or a place to live in permanently?
Or perhaps a mixture of the two: a holiday home now, eventually to become a place to retire to.

Do you plan to spend merely a longish summer holiday there, or are you hoping to get there for frequent weekend breaks?
The answer to this question will have a bearing on where you decide to buy. If your French property is to be used only for an annual summer holiday, it can be more or less anywhere in France: you don't need to worry about how long it takes to get there. Indeed, part of the delight of owning your own place in France may be a long, slow car journey by stages across the country, stopping off for delicious meals and a night or two in peaceful country hotels on the way. You need not worry about heating either: an open fire to take the chill off on cooler evenings will be enough.

On the other hand you will have to give careful thought to what will happen to the place during the rest of the year. Unless you are buying a large house or château and plan to keep resident domestic help, or at any rate to have a cleaning lady and gardener who will come in regularly, you may need to find someone to keep an eye on it. This will not necessarily be easy, especially in the depths of the country. Any furniture you put in it must be capable of withstanding unheated winter conditions. You will probably have to take bedding and linen home for the winter. You will have to consider potential problems like frost and frozen pipes. You will probably not be able to keep a garden going unless you pay someone to water it and to keep it under control: many a holiday-home owner has had to get hold of a scythe to cope with the results of spring and early summer growth. I have a vivid memory of going on holiday for just two weeks in early June when I lived in the Touraine and coming back to find the garden a jungle, the grass far too high to mow.

If your aim is to get away for frequent breaks, your priorities will be different. Access must be quick to make it worthwhile. Hence the large number of British people who have bought near the Channel ports, and within easy reach of the exit from the Channel Tunnel. But quick access does not necessarily mean nearby. If you are prepared to fly-and-drive, you have a much wider choice. Anywhere within easy reach of, say, Bordeaux or Nice, Nantes or Toulouse airports becomes a possibility. But you should bear in mind that car hire is expensive in France. (Some home-owners in Languedoc and Roussillon fly to Barcelona and hire a car in Spain, where it is considerably cheaper.) And you will also need to check convenience of flights. Some destinations are geared chiefly to business travellers and are poorly served, or not served at all, at weekends. Others are frequently booked up, or are very expensive (London–Nice is a notorious example). Yet others operate only in the summer months.

France's rail network is excellent, but again you need to look into convenience of service. Areas now served by the high-speed train (TGV) lines have become much more accessible for short breaks, but places off main lines may have infrequent services that are hard to combine with flights from Britain. You must also bear in mind that seats on TGVs have to be booked in advance – not an easy matter if you are just popping over for a long weekend.

The next chapter gives you some examples of the accessibility of certain regions. Don't forget that if you hope to have friends and family to stay, ease of access will probably be important to them too.

Are you planning to retire there one day?

I don't want to be ageist about this, but do bear in mind that when you are older you will probably want somewhere reasonably close to shops and perhaps to doctors. If you are a couple and plan to spend the whole of your old age there, you must consider that one of you will probably die first and the other will not want to be too isolated. You will no doubt hope that your children and grandchildren will come to stay often, so somewhere accessible may mean more frequent visits.

Are you hoping to make a profit on reselling?

The advice from experts is, forget it! Although prices have gone up in some areas of France, partly as a result of foreign buyers, it has on the whole been from a very low base. For instance, prices did certainly rise substantially in the area close to the Channel Tunnel as a result of the boom caused in the late eighties by the British rushing there to buy old farmhouses and some coastal property. But prices had previously been depressed by the closure of traditional industries. And the boom was relatively short-lived, as buyers decided to go further afield.

Basically, with the exception of Paris (where prices in fact went down in the early nineties) and the Côte d'Azur, there has never been the sort of price explosion seen in Britain during the seventies and eighties. Prices have risen on average by 3, 4, perhaps 5 per cent a year from time immemorial, more or less in line with inflation. Even where factors such as the arrival of a new high-speed train service, putting a town in, say, commuting distance of Paris, were expected to push prices up, the effect has been much less significant than anticipated, thanks to the recession.

Moreover, the system of property purchasing in France means that you must pay another 12–15 per cent of the purchase price on top, to cover legal fees, taxes and agent's commission – or even as much as 20 per cent if you take out a mortgage. It will therefore take you a long time to get back to square one, let alone start making a profit (see Chapter 3). Another important factor is that the French tax system discourages property speculation. Chapter 8 explains how capital gains tax is payable on second homes by both residents and non-residents; it is payable even on main residences if you move within two years, except in special circumstances.

So the chances of your making a real profit in the short term are minimal, and remain slim even in the medium term. You should also bear in mind that renovated country places are not on the whole popular with the

French, who are more likely to go for seaside flats or villas, or for flats and chalets in ski resorts. So if you want to sell on, your main potential market will be either British, or people from elsewhere in northern Europe.

Are you hoping to make an income from letting or offering bed-and-breakfast?
Here, too, you must think carefully. You could probably make an income from a small flat in a city like Montpellier or Toulouse, since you could let year-round. But you would need to appoint someone to manage your flat, and you would have to be very careful, since the law firmly protects tenants' rights, and you might have trouble getting rid of unwanted tenants. Holiday lets are a possible source of income in many areas, but only for a few months in the year, and many areas favoured by the British are not likely to appeal to French holidaymakers. This applies particularly to rural areas. Coastal flats and mountain chalets stand a better chance of being let to the French.

Bed-and-breakfast is unlikely to make you much of an income, though it may cover some of the renovation costs of turning an outbuilding into a *gîte* (see Chapter 7).

Key question 2:
Do you want a house or a flat?
The advantage of a flat is that it will almost certainly be in a block or a new development, with a *gardien* or janitor to take in your post and, if given a large enough tip from time to time, to keep an eye on it when you are away. There will be no garden to worry about either. Flats are normally bought *en copropriété*, which means much the same as what is called in the United States a condominium. Basically, you own your own flat, but on top of that you have a share (depending roughly on the size and value of the flat) in the common parts. In a new development or renovated block this might include a swimming pool and landscaped gardens. In an older block it will simply be stairs and entrance hall. A long list of owners' obligations to their fellow owners is set out in a fat document called the *règlement de copropriété*, which includes the share of the service charges you will have to pay. It is all quite complicated but well organised, with a *syndic*, a person nominated by the co-owners, to look after the management of the whole *copropriété*, usually for a limited term, and prepare its accounts.

Buying a house is very different. You will have to think about who will keep an eye on it when you aren't there, decide what to do about a garden, see if you can find someone to check whether there is any post for you and so on. There are now a number of people advertising services designed to deal with such problems as looking after gardens, checking up on the house, or draining the swimming pool at the end of the summer. If you become friendly with the neighbours this will help the situation too.

Key question 3:
Old property or new?

You need to think about what will suit you best. A modern flat or house with plenty of mod cons but perhaps little character. Or an old house that may have plenty of character but needs substantial renovation, or that has been modernised to a standard that isn't your own. The French have an expression: '*Quand le bâtiment va, tout va*' ('When the construction industry is flourishing, everything's going fine'). To encourage this happy state of affairs, there are tax advantages to buying new property (which means less than five years old). This is another factor you might like to consider.

Key question 4:
In town, village or country, or in a resort?

The answer to this question will depend partly on how much time you intend to spend in France. The countryside and seaside resorts can seem pretty bleak in winter, even in the south, but will be delightful for a summer holiday. Although many British people start off by thinking they want to be in the depths of the country, they are liable to change their mind when they see how far they have to drive for a box of matches. France is a big country and distances can be great in the countryside. A house on the outskirts of a village may be more suitable – near shops and other amenities, but still peaceful and rural. And a house in a small village may have a number of advantages: a manageable garden, for instance. Agents report that many British clients say they want plenty of land, but then realise that it is not easy to look after – you don't want to spend all your holidays with a scythe at the ready.

You need to think in the long term too. You may now have small children, who will love being in the middle of the countryside, thrilled at being able to explore outbuildings, climb trees, fish or swim in the local stream. But in a few years' time they will turn into easily bored teenagers, more interested in the bright lights. If you hope for family holidays continuing until they are virtually grown up, with their friends joining you, you should consider being in a small town, or even in a quiet part of a largish town. That way you won't find yourself landed with sulky youngsters – or spend half your time driving all over the countryside collecting them from cinemas or discos.

I've always thought that the tall house I lived in for a while in Tours would have made an ideal holiday home for a British family. It was in a quiet leafy area but only ten minutes' walk from the town centre and the station, with plenty of space for everyone to do their own thing, a pretty walled garden, a big cellar and lots of character. There were people all round to keep an eye on things, lovely countryside nearby, excellent restaurants in and outside the town, and plenty of things to do with visitors without having to drive for miles. That doesn't, of course, correspond to the classic dream of a rustic farmhouse or a charming cottage or an elegant manor house. But I suggest that a town house might be a solution that would provide happy family holidays and short breaks for many years. Prices in provincial towns are mostly low by the standards of southern England and you'd encounter few difficulties in selling that sort of house, whereas a place in the country is not always easy to sell.

Beware distances!
Unless you live in parts of Scotland or Wales, you won't be used to the vast open spaces of France! You need to do some adjusting as you decide on the type of property that will suit you.

'Living in the country here isn't like being five miles outside Taunton,' remarked a British journalist and teacher now living in the Lot and working for an estate agent, showing would-be British buyers over property in the area. 'It's more like being in the wilds of Scotland. And with winding roads you can take much longer than you'd imagine from looking at the map.'

If you think you want to escape from the stresses of urban living and enjoy the peace of the countryside, remember that in France you may be 20 kilometres from the nearest shop or café, even from the nearest house – a factor to be reckoned with if you forget to buy bread or need a doctor in a hurry. Another English employee of an agency in the Lot commented that he had got used to people announcing: 'I want to be completely isolated', but changing their minds when they realised just how isolated, many of the local cottages are. Another agent specialising in northern France told of a young couple who asked for a tiny cottage in the middle of a field, but whose faces fell when they discovered that there were no shops for miles and ended up delighted with a little house in a busy street in a fishing harbour. 'Most people end up wanting to be near facilities, even if they think they don't at the outset,' adds Vivian Bridge of Northern France Properties.* And an agent in the south-west emphasised that he found his British clients particularly bad at judging distances: 'They seem to be really thrown by so much empty space and can't get their bearings.'

Key question 5:
Are you prepared to do substantial renovation?
Do think hard about this if you have read about the amazingly low prices in France for charming country cottages. You can indeed find cottages for £20,000. You can even find cottages and barns for as little as £7,000. But none of them is in a state to move into. You will have to do very substantial renovation, probably including installing a drainage system, electricity and water for that price. If you are prepared to spend a lot of time and money well and good. Or you may be willing to camp out there for a while, doing it up gradually. But you must be sure that you really want to launch into such an undertaking, and that you have the time to cope with it. See Chapter 5 for some costs, and some hints about renovating and restoring country places.

Key question 6:
Are you planning a classic purchase, or do you want to look into the possibility of other methods?

Leaseback
One of these is a sale-and-leaseback scheme. The basic system is that you buy a property – generally a flat or house in a new development – at a 30 per cent discount and then lease it back to the property company for eleven years. During that period you don't pay any service or maintenance charges, not even the insurance or electricity bills, but you can use it free of charge for your own holidays, for about six weeks a year. It won't be suitable if you want to be able to pop over for the weekend, as you have to give your holiday dates in advance (generally a mixture of high and low season), although you aren't committed to the same period year after year. At the end of the eleven years the lease expires and, as you own the freehold, you are free to occupy it full-time if you want to. The system is recognized and protected by French law and many people find it a good method if they are intending to retire to France: it gives them a chance to acclimatize themselves to the area during their holidays there at different times of year, before moving in permanently when the lease expires.

Buying through a company
French companies set up for the purpose of buying property are called *sociétés civiles immobilières* or SCI. Many British people are interested in this type of ownership structure because it avoids the effects of France's inheritance regulations, which are quite different from those in Britain (see Chapter 3). If you own shares in an SCI you can dispose of them in accordance with English law, or the law of anywhere else you may be domiciled. But this doesn't mean your heirs won't have to pay inheritance duties in France – whether or not you are a French resident, they will have to pay duty on your French assets. Sales of shares in an SCI involve much lower legal fees than ordinary property sales, which is an added attraction. However the registration fees for setting up the company in the first place are high.

The SCI formula may be worth considering if, say, you are thinking of buying a French home with another family. But it is essential to pay for expert legal and financial advice before embarking on any such step.

Joint buying
Another way of mitigating the effects of inheritance laws can be to buy jointly, a method known as *en tontine*. It is, however, a very complex issue, and one that can be fraught with difficulties, not least because once done it is virtually impossible to unscramble it – a big disadvantage in the case of, say, a divorce. The basic principle is that when the first of the joint buyers dies, the house or flat is treated as having been the property of the surviving owner or owners. Although this can help to mitigate the effects

of French inheritance legislation, once again it does not mean that inheritance duties can be avoided. Again, you must take good legal and financial advice.

Key question 7:
How much are you prepared to pay?
An obvious question, but one that you must think about carefully before you start looking for a house or flat. Before you answer it, read Chapter 3 to understand what you will be paying on top of the selling price, and the information on mortgages in this chapter. Do also take account of any renovation work you may have to do.

Understanding the money
Discussing figures in a foreign language is always something of a nightmare. And even when you have asked for the various figures to be written down, there are two important points to remember. The basic key is to tell yourself that **a full stop means a comma** and **a comma means a full stop**, and that **a space means a comma**.

Thus *100.000* in French would be written in English as *100,000*. So *100.000* francs (or sometimes *FF 100.000*) means a hundred thousand francs. This may also be expressed as *100 000* francs, without the full stop.

On the other hand, decimal points are written in French as commas. So 3,5% is the French equivalent of 3.5% in English.

Converting prices
As a quick, rough-and-ready conversion rate from francs to pounds, most British visitors to France used simply to divide by ten. But since sterling's departure from the ERM and its subsequent slide against other currencies, it is essential that you should check what the current exchange rate is. While no one will be able to tell you what the rate will be in a couple of months' time, when you have to produce the money – if prediction was that easy, all financial advisers would be millionaires – it is certainly worth watching the way the exchange rate is going. If during that period the exchange rate becomes particularly favourable (i.e. if the pound is higher than average against the franc), you might think it worth transferring pounds into francs in advance of the sale date. But you must take advice from your accountant or bank manager on this, as loss of interest at home may outweigh any exchange rate gain.

Beware old francs!
So-called 'new francs' (*nouveaux francs*) were introduced into France as long ago as 1959. But it is a curious fact that over thirty years after their official disappearance, 'old francs' (*anciens francs*) have by no means vanished from everyday vocabulary. And even those who were not yet born when the change was made have picked up the habits of their parents and grandparents and may talk in old francs in certain cases.

Unfortunately the most common case is when talking of property prices. It is therefore essential that you should read the following paragraph very carefully.

One new franc replaced a hundred old francs. Therefore a million old francs is the equivalent of 10,000 new francs. When speaking of property prices, ordinary French people are liable to refer to a house worth, say, 50 million: i.e. 50 million old francs (or 500,000 new francs). Agents and *notaires* used to dealing with foreigners are unlikely to do so. But those whose clients are mostly locals, especially in the depths of the country, may inadvertently slip into old francs. And you may find yourself discussing with a seller direct, or perhaps asking the local farmer whether a piece of land adjoining your prospective purchase is going to come on the market and if so at what price. There is a good chance that old francs will be used here.

Moreover, the media know that many of their readers or listeners or viewers still think in terms of old francs. As the government frowns on their perpetuating the practice, they get round the problem by referring to 'twenty million centimes' (i.e. 20 million old francs or 200,000 new francs).

In case you think I am exaggerating, let me tell you a story which appeared in the French press only a couple of years ago. A fairly elderly aristocrat gave a cheque to his gardener when he left his service. He meant to make him a present of what was then about £500. But instead of writing 5,000 francs, he wrote 500 000 francs – giving the gardener a princely £50,000. The delighted gardener paid it in. And when his ex-employer realised what he had done, he refused to pay it back. The case eventually came to court and the magistrate found for the gardener, saying that the cheque was valid as it was written, whatever the writer's intention.

Key question 8:
To mortgage or not to mortgage?
It is particularly important to think this question out well in advance of finding a property you want to buy. The reason for this is simple: when you sign the preliminary contract to purchase the property, which necessitates putting down a deposit of at least 5 per cent and probably 10 per cent of the purchase price, you will be asked whether or not you intend to take out a mortgage or bank loan to pay for the property.

The full procedure is explained in Chapter 3, but you must be aware at this early stage that the preliminary contract is binding, and the deposit non-returnable – except that it may be subject to certain conditions. One of these conditions can be your ability to obtain a loan. Then if you can't for some reason get the loan you had hoped for, the contract becomes null and void and you can recover your deposit.

BUT if you say at the outset that you do not intend to seek a loan, you will have to add a rider to the contract – in your own writing to impress its importance on you – saying that you are aware that if you change your mind and do after all seek a loan, failing to obtain one will *not* be considered to be a reason for your getting out of the contract and recovering your deposit. It is vital that you are ready to answer this question of a loan when the time comes.

If you have the choice between financing out of your own resources or borrowing, the first questions you must ask yourself are the same as those you would ask if you were buying property in Britain. And if you have an accountant you would be well advised to consult him/her about the relative merits of having capital free to invest, or perhaps to use for renovations to the property. But remember that on this occasion there is no question of tax relief: even if you have no mortgage on your permanent home, the Inland Revenue does not allow tax relief on second homes, nor indeed on any property abroad.

Another factor to take into account is the cost of buying a property with a mortgage. As well as the arrangement and valuation fees usually charged by the lender, you will have to pay extra legal fees on the purchase. On top of that the lawyer handling the conveyancing must collect a recording tax based on the size of the mortgage, plus in some cases an additional fee of about the same again. He/she may also charge for expenses involved in completing the mortgage formalities. So one way or another, it is quite an expensive business.

Finding a mortgage
The volatile situation created by the withdrawal of sterling and some other currencies from the Exchange-Rate Mechanism meant that the question of where best to apply for a mortgage for a French purchase became more complex. It must also be said that a number of lenders, particularly banks and other institutions in France, had their fingers burnt when some of their British clients defaulted on their repayments, leaving them with a virtually unsaleable 'wreck' in many cases. The French have traditionally been more responsible in their borrowings than the British – and to be fair have not been encouraged by lenders to over-commit themselves, as has happened in Britain. French banks and other lenders therefore accepted borrowers' statements about their ability to repay at face value. They have now learnt through experience to be more careful. And some French banks have simply stopped lending to the British.

You may well find it difficult to borrow on very low-priced properties in need of total renovation. Some lenders stipulate that properties must have electricity, drainage and water, or even fully equipped bathrooms – so that if the worst comes to the worst they will at least have a relatively saleable commodity on their hands.

In sterling or francs?
You may have little choice here. The sharp drop in value of the pound, and the uncertainty surrounding its future within or outside the ERM, scared off some lenders in sterling. If you are buying, say, a pricey villa on

the Côte d'Azur you probably won't experience any difficulty in finding a sterling mortgage. But for cheap rural properties it may be considerably more difficult. If you do have a choice, you must look into such matters as interest rates (traditionally lower in France, but not in the aftermath of the sterling plunge against other currencies). The choice must also depend on where you are earning the money that will be used for the repayments. For instance at least some of it may be coming from rent received on your French home, or bed-and-breakfast income (though do make sure not to overestimate this). Advice from an impartial expert, geared to your personal financial and family circumstances, is to be recommended, especially in a time of uncertainty in foreign exchange markets.

Or in another currency?
It may be possible to take out a mortgage in, say, Swiss francs or Japanese yen, or indeed in Ecus. But you must bear in mind that while interest rates may be lower, you are at the mercy of a drop in the value of the pound against the mortgage currency (which makes the repayments more expensive) and in that of the franc against the mortgage currency (which means that the value of your French home is eroded). Expert advice is essential here.

Fixed or variable rate?
French property loans were traditionally offered only at an interest rate that remained fixed throughout the term of the loan – the French, unlike the British, are not natural gamblers. However some lenders do now offer variable-rate franc mortgages: the rate is revised annually in line with current bank rates, but there may be a maximum percentage change in either direction (i.e. it cannot go up or down more than an agreed percentage), and there may be an initial period during which the rate cannot be changed. It may be possible to change from a fixed-rate to a variable-rate mortgage. But early repayment is liable to incur a penalty, at any rate on fixed-rate loans. However if you sell your French home and buy another one, it may well be possible to transfer the mortgage.

Other conditions
You cannot usually commit yourself to repayments higher than one-third of gross monthly income in France, and when calculating the maximum loan they can offer, lenders will also take into account any mortgage commitments you may have on your British home. Lenders will probably insist on a valuation (which you will have to pay for) and will not lend more than 70 to 80 per cent of that valuation (or of the purchase price, excluding commission, fees and taxes, if it is lower). There is usually a minimum advance, and some lenders have minimum annual income requirements, which may vary depending on which part of France you are buying in. Expect to have to take out life insurance; the premiums will probably be included in the monthly repayment figure.

Secured on your British or French home?

If you are offered a choice, you may feel the easiest solution is to increase your existing British mortgage, or remortage your home in Britain. But then if the worst happens and you cannot keep up with the repayments, you are putting your permanent home at risk. If the mortgage is secured on your French holiday home that potential problem is avoided.

While on this topic, I should point out that it is not unknown for a British lender to attempt to obtain repossession of a French home if the owners fall behind with repayments on a mortgage on their British residence. So do make sure not to over-commit yourself.

What extras are involved?

A valuation fee will be charged by French lenders. There may also be an arrangement fee.

A look at lenders

Because of problems encountered with some British borrowers, the choice of mortgages on offer is not as wide as it was at the beginning of the nineties. Both **Barclays** and the **National Westminster** offer mortgages on French property via their French subsidiaries. The French bank **Crédit agricole** has a scheme called *Mortgage à la française*, while **UCB** (Union de Crédit pour le Bâtiment) offers *Crédit Diapason*. The **Crédit Lyonnais** and **BNP** (Banque nationale de Paris) are still offering mortgages on French homes, and so is the **Banque transatlantique**, though after some bad experiences with British borrowers it is being particularly cautious and may inquire into your income before sending information.

Two subsidiaries of British building societies are also in the market. The Abbey National, which bought a French home loans company in 1990, have renamed it **Abbey National France**. Contact them for details of their French mortgage scheme at the French address below. The Woolwich building society's subsidiary is simply called **Banque Woolwich**. Again, contact them in France. Both companies have English-speaking staff and information packs in English.

Ordinary bank loans

If you have decided to rent a *gîte* a few times before you take the plunge to buy your own place, you might consider starting a savings scheme tied to a property loan with a local bank. French banks have schemes called a *compte d'épargne logement* and a *plan d'épargne logement* under which you can only obtain a loan after a certain length of time. As this also represents a way of saving, it might be worth looking into. Interest rates are normally lower than on a full-scale mortgage once you reach the loan stage. However, such loans are not always available for second homes.

Renovation mortgages
You may be able to borrow in order to carry out renovation or restoration of an old property. In some cases you can even borrow after the event, usually within six months of the work being completed. You will need to produce detailed estimates or receipts and possibly architect's drawings if it is a major conversion.

Documentation required
French banks require what seem like mountains of paperwork along with the application form for the loan. They generally ask for a photocopy of the first five pages of your passport and a birth certificate, plus proof that your permanent residence is in Britain. You'll need to send along a copy of the preliminary purchase agreement, recent payslips and tax returns (or accountant's letter if you're self-employed) and evidence of your existing mortgage commitments if any.

Contact addresses for requesting documentation

Abbey National France
BP 219
1461 av. du Cateau
59404 Cambrai Cedex
France
tel: (010-33) 27-73-33-40
fax: (010-33) 27-73-33-01

Banque nationale de Paris (BNP)
Knollys House
47 Mark Lane
London EC3R 7QH
tel: 071-380 5019

Banque transatlantique
36 St James's Street
London SW1A 1JD
tel: 071-493 6717
fax: 071-495 1018

Banque Woolwich
34 blvd Malesherbes
75008 Paris
France
tel: (010-33-1) 47-42-70-89
fax: (010-33-1) 47-42-90-14

Barclays
ask at your local branch

Crédit agricole
Mortgage à la française
Spencer House
29 Sheen Road
Richmond TW9 1BN
tel: 081-332-0096/7
fax: 081-332-0098

Crédit Lyonnais
French Mortgage Department
84–94 Queen Victoria Street
London EC4P 4LX
tel: 071-634 8068
fax: 071-329-4322

National Westminster
ask at your local branch

UCB
Cellule britannique
25 av. Kléber
75116 Paris Cedex
France
tel: (010-33-1) 40-67-42-91

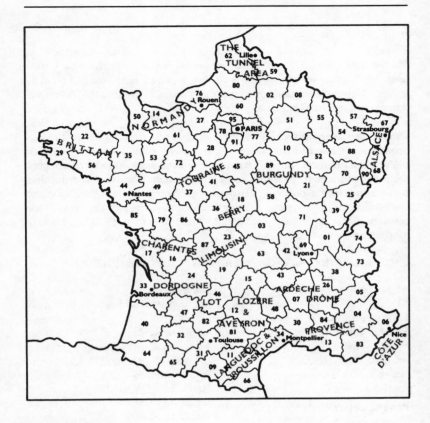

French Départements

01	Ain	26	Drôme	52	Haute-Marne	78	Yvelines
02	Aisne	27	Eure	53	Mayenne	79	Deux-Sèvres
03	Allier	28	Eure-et-Loir	54	Meurthe-et-Moselle	80	Somme
04	Alpes-de-Haute-	29	Finistère	55	Meuse	81	Tarn
	Provence	30	Gard	56	Morbihan	82	Tarn-et-Garonne
05	Hautes-Alpes	31	Haute-Garonne	57	Moselle	83	Var
06	Alpes-Maritimes	32	Gers	58	Nièvre	84	Vaucluse
07	Ardèche	33	Gironde	59	Nord	85	Vendée
08	Ardennes	34	Hérault	60	Oise	86	Vienne
09	Ariège	35	Ille-et-Vilaine	61	Orne	87	Haute-Vienne
10	Aube	36	Indre	62	Pas-de-Calais	88	Vosges
11	Aude	37	Indre-et-Loire	63	Puy-de-Dôme	89	Yonne
12	Aveyron	38	Isère	64	Pyrénées-Atlantiques	90	Belfort
13	Bouches-du-Rhône	39	Jura	65	Hautes-Pyrénées		
14	Calvados	40	Landes	66	Pyrénées-Orientales	**Paris area**	
15	Cantal	41	Loir-et-Cher	67	Bas-Rhin		
16	Charente	42	Loire	68	Haut-Rhin	91	Essonne
17	Charente-Maritime	43	Haute-Loire	69	Rhône	92	Hauts-de-Seine
18	Cher	44	Loire-Atlantique	70	Haute-Saône	93	Seine-Saint-Denis
19	Corrèze	45	Loiret	71	Saône-et-Loire	94	Val-de-Marne
20	Corse	46	Lot	72	Sarthe	95	Val-d'Oise
21	Côte d'Or	47	Lot-et-Garonne	73	Savoie		
22	Côte d'Armor	48	Lozère	74	Haute-Savoie		
23	Creuse	49	Maine-et-Loire	75	Paris		
24	Dordogne	50	Manche	76	Seine-Maritime		
25	Doubs	51	Marne	77	Seine-et-Marne		

2 CHOOSING THE REGION

You may already be particularly familiar with one region of France and now feel that you would like a home of your own there. But otherwise you will need to do some research into the various regions to see what best suits the needs and priorities you have established after answering the key questions in Chapter 1.

The map opposite shows the ninety-five French *départements* (roughly equivalent to a county) within each region, each of which has a number that features on the postcode and on car number plates. Tourist literature, a useful starting point for your research once you have narrowed the choice down a bit, is supplied both by regional tourist offices and by departmental offices. To complicate matters, the old names of provinces or regions are still widely used. For instance, the Dordogne is referred to by the locals as Périgord, the Lot as Quercy.

In a book of this size I cannot go into detail about every region of France. I have therefore started with some general information about climate, access, types of property and prices, then highlighted areas currently popular with British buyers, with brief information in each case about landscape and climate, access, types and prices of property available, popularity with French and foreign buyers, cultural and culinary interest. A section on areas long popular with Francophiles follows, and the chapter ends with a few lesser-known regions that are worth looking at, plus a brief look at Paris.

I have included tourist information offices and suggestions for further reading for the main areas. Detailed maps of France can be obtained from major bookshops with map and guide departments, and from **Stanford's**, 12–14 Long Acre, London WC2E 9LP (tel: 071-836 1321), which also has a large selection of travel and guide books, as do **Daunt Books**, 83 Marylebone High St, London W1 4DE (tel: 071-224 2295) and **The Travel Bookshop**, 13 Blenheim Crescent, London W11 2EE (tel: 071-229 5260), both a good source of out-of-print books as they have second-hand sections. Also **Travellers Bookshop**, 25 Cecil Court, London WC2N 4EZ (tel: 071-836 9132). **Compass Books**, 15 Bertie Ward Way, Dereham, Norfolk NR19 1TE (tel: Dereham (0362) 691 623, fax: Dereham (0362 691 108) offer a mail-order service; they can give advice about books about France and supply lists on request.

Climate

French weather forecasters traditionally divide France into 'north of the Loire' and 'south of the Loire'. As a rough rule of thumb, the weather north of the Loire is fairly similar to that in southern England, while there is a perceptible difference to the south. Another rule of thumb: western regions are on the whole wetter than eastern.

You would expect the whole of southern France to have hot summers. But remember that whereas nowhere in Britain is far from the sea, France, in spite of its long and varied coastline, has many landlocked areas that enjoy what is referred to as a 'continental climate'. The summer months are, for instance, very hot in Alsace, Burgundy and the Touraine. The winters are different though: mainly dry and very cold in Alsace, foggy and quite cold in Burgundy, mild and damp in the Touraine.

British people living in what is basically, despite recent aberrations, a temperate climate, need to adjust their thinking if they opt for a region with a more extreme climate. Many people discovered in the long hot summers of 1989 and 1990 that they didn't like the heat as much as they thought – and found gardening a nightmare. And regions that are hot in summer often have surprisingly cold winters, and fierce rainstorms at certain times of year. Make sure that you are going to be able to cope with these extremes. If you do decide to buy in just such a region, be prepared for frequent maintenance work. For instance, the blistering summer sun will mean that your smartly stripped shutters will need revarnishing every year. Your cellar may well flood from time to time too. Before you plan to turn it into a rumpus area for children, full of amusing floor cushions, remember that you will need to get everything into an upstairs room before you shut the place up for the winter – better still, take it all home with you.

Such problems are not likely to arise in the north, but you do need to think about climate here too. If you complain about the British climate, you may feel it doesn't make sense to opt for something similar in France. A region like the Touraine or southern Brittany, with milder winters but not too far from Britain, might suit you better.

One more tip: when you are visiting a potential region, keep an ear open for labels attached to regions or towns, as they are often revealing. The Loire Valley châteaux area, for instance, is frequently referred to as the 'Garden of France'. Now gardens need watering, so this is a pointer to a humid climate, with plenty of summer rain. The much less complimentary nickname for Rouen, *le pot de chambre de la Normandie* (Normandy's chamber pot), again tells you that rainfall is high there.

Another factor to take into account is wind. The *mistral*, which blows fiercely in the Rhône delta and up the Rhône Valley, produces brilliantly blue skies on the Côte d'Azur and in Provence, but can be bitterly cold and sets many people's nerves on edge. Further west in Languedoc and Roussillon the cold *tramontane* can make life unpleasant.

Prices

A rough guide to prices in the various most popular regions is included in this chapter, but in general terms it can be said that the boom in demand from British property buyers did not push prices up substantially. M. Dubuc,* a Norman agent, says that although prices did rise very slight-ly as a result of the expansion of the market that started in late 1988 and early 1989, two factors prevented any dramatic rises. Firstly, the sheer number of houses on the market at the time, which easily outstripped demand. Secondly, although that initial boom did certainly mean that a number of properties that had been on his books for some time were sold, they were soon replaced as the locals read articles in the press about the British 'invasion' and decided to cash in: new properties suddenly started flooding in as people remembered their old granny's cottage or a disused barn in one of their fields.

British interest in the Lot probably resulted in a price rise of about 15 per cent, according to Francis Puche at the Crédit Agricole in Cahors, but, he adds, 'don't forget they were starting from an awfully low base in this basically poor area'.

Vivian Bridge at Northern France Properties* reckons that there was a rise of something like 30 per cent in the Pas-de-Calais area near the Channel Tunnel exit. But again he points out that this was from a low base: prices had been falling for some eight years before the British boom started in 1988, as a result of the decline of the traditional industries, widespread unemployment and the resulting loss in purchasing power.

Sterling's departure from the ERM in 1992 and subsequent sharp drop against the French franc inevitably had an effect on prices achieved in areas popular with the British, though asking prices remained the same. However many rural places had not been lived in for years, or even centuries, and their French owners were usually in no particular hurry to sell, so preferred to wait till the sterling/franc rate improved rather than dropping the price. Other factors have played a part in prices too: for instance in the ski resorts in the Roussillon area, Spaniards have been buying on a big scale, pushing prices up. In Paris, prices have dropped for the first time for many years, but they remain very high, and despite the recession, demand for luxury villas on the Côte d'Azur has generally held up.

Nevertheless, in a time of Europe-wide recession, property has generally become something of a buyer's market. But you should see this as enabling you to proceed cautiously and at your own pace, rather than as a time for finding bargains (unless you are buying from a British family hard-hit by the recession at home).

Access

France's good motorway network means that you can travel about the country reasonably fast, although the A6/A7 route to the south coast becomes notoriously congested and accident-prone at weekends and throughout the summer holiday period. Nevertheless it is a large country and you should not underestimate the time needed to reach your prospective holiday home, especially when driving in summer heat. Nor should you underestimate the cost of travelling on motorways, most of which are toll roads. Some motorways now bear differing tolls depending on the time of day. Other main roads are generally well maintained, but often carry heavy traffic, with mobile homes a particular problem in the summer. High petrol costs should also be taken into account.

If you plan well in advance, you can save a lot of tiring driving by using the efficient overnight Motorail service: you put the car on the train and travel overnight in a couchette, then enjoy breakfast at your destination, courtesy of the railways, while the car is being unloaded. There are services from Calais to destinations like Avignon (useful for Provence and the Ardèche), Biarritz, Bordeaux and Brive (for the southwest), Fréjus and Nice (for the Côte d'Azur and Provence), Narbonne (for Languedoc and Roussillon, and Lozère and Aveyron) and Toulouse (for the southwest). Also Dieppe to Avignon. A number of destinations are served from Paris, including Nice and Toulouse, that allow you to travel separately from your car and therefore book a sleeper rather than a couchette. Bicycles can be carried on some services too. AA Motoring Services, Motorail and P & O European Ferries offer packages from Britain covering the Channel crossing, the train journey for both you and the car, plus insurance.

A number of provincial airports in France are served by direct flights from London, some of them seasonal, and Nice, Bordeaux and Lyon also have direct flights from Manchester, while Nice is also served direct from Birmingham (seasonal). At the time of writing, you can fly direct to France from the following British airports, but since the Gulf War brought tourist figures crashing downwards, airlines have been constantly cancelling and adding routes, so you must check the current position: Aberdeen, Birmingham, Bristol, Cardiff, East Midlands, Edinburgh, Glasgow, Jersey, Leeds/Bradford, all four London airports, Manchester, Newcastle, Southampton. From Paris, the main French internal carrier *Air Inter* provides extensive service all over the country, so you should still be able to arrange air travel to the nearest French airport to your new French home. See information on individual regions later in this chapter to find out which French airports will be most convenient. Some flights do not operate all year. Fly-and-drive packages are available to many destinations and *Air France* and the SNCF (French Rail) offer good-value combined air and rail journeys from Britain to any one of several thousand French stations.

Rail plus car or bike hire packages have long been available from the SNCF, one of the world's most efficient and extensive rail networks. High-speed trains (*trains à grande vitesse* or TGV), for which seats must be booked, have cut travelling time dramatically to the south and now to the west as well (and will link with the Channel Tunnel in due course), but ordinary expresses are also excellent: fast, comfortable and reliable. Prices are reasonable, too, especially if you can avoid travelling between Friday and Saturday lunchtime and on Sunday afternoons and evenings and Monday mornings. There are numerous reductions on offer (for couples, students and several members of the same family travelling together outside peak times). The over-sixties can travel at half-price outside peak times if they buy a modestly priced *Carte Vermeil*. Rail Rover tickets (*France Vacances*) are good value if you plan to do a lot of rail travel over a short period. Overnight services with couchettes and sleepers run to most distant destinations, but the TGVs do not operate at night.

Ferry crossings
In the run-up to the opening of the Channel Tunnel in 1994, there is increasing competition on fares and other benefits from the various ferry and hovercraft or Seacat companies, which also offer special all-in rates for short trips that may be useful if you're on a brief househunting expedition by car.

Working westwards, you can cross from Ramsgate to Dunkirk (Sally Ferries), Dover to Calais (Stena Sealink, P&O, Hoverspeed), Dover to Boulogne (Hoverspeed), Folkestone to Boulogne (Hoverspeed), Newhaven to Dieppe (Stena Sealink), Portsmouth to Le Havre (P & O), Caen/Ouistreham (Brittany Ferries), Southampton to Cherbourg (Stena Sealink), Saint-Malo (Brittany Ferries), Poole to Cherbourg (Brittany Ferries), and Plymouth to Roscoff (Brittany Ferries).

Also available are services from the Channel Islands to Saint-Malo (Commodore, Emeraude Ferries), as well as catamarans to Saint-Quay-Portrieux, and from Cork to Roscoff (Brittany Ferries), Cherbourg and Le Havre (Irish Ferries), as well as Rosslare to Cherbourg and Le Havre (Irish Ferries).

French property owners club
Once you have bought your house or flat in France you can save on travelling costs by joining Brittany Ferries' French Property Owners Club, which entitles you to up to 30 per cent discounts year-round on passenger and car single fares on most Brittany Ferries crossings from Portsmouth to Caen and Saint-Malo, from Plymouth to Roscoff and from Poole to Cherbourg. You can also benefit from 10 per cent discounts on five-day excursion return fares (passengers and cars) and on restaurant meals and wine on board. The club also operates a system of 'guest party' vouchers which you can give to people holidaying in your house or flat: the whole party travelling together can save 15 per cent on most Channel crossings (again both passengers and car).

You pay a registration fee (£30 in 1993) and an annual subscription. Write for a membership application form to French Property Owners Club, Brittany Ferries, Freepost, Plymouth PL1 1BR or telephone Plymouth (0752) 226076.

The monthly *French Property News* has opened its own club, called French Property News Travel Club. It offers members vouchers redeemable against holiday bookings, discounts on air fares as well as ferry tickets to France, and on many air fares and travel packages worldwide, car hire, travel and car breakdown insurance and holidays and coach tours, plus a variety of special offers, weekend breaks and the like. Membership in 1993 cost £10. Write to French Property News, 2a Lambton Road, London SW20 0LR for application form.

Be realistic about travelling times

Even the least pushy agent is prone to wild optimism when it comes to the question of how long it will take you to reach your dream holiday home. I have seen many a brochure claiming, say, that Tours would be only four hours' drive from London once the Channel Tunnel was open. A look at the map will show you that this cannot be true, even when you can use the motorway from Calais to Rouen.

At the time of writing, the Channel Tunnel was not yet open. If all goes according to plan, by the middle of 1994 journey time to France by car will have been substantially reduced. Train passengers will have to wait until the high-speed train service to Calais opens (probably mid-1990s) to start feeling the full benefits, and the much-hyped 'only three hours from London to Paris by train' remains a distant dream (British Rail is talking of a high-speed link from London to the Channel coast by the end of the century). Meanwhile, current accessibility should be examined carefully. It is, for instance, true that you can get to the area round Rouen from London in about seven hours, if you time the ferry crossing carefully. But if you try to take a weekend break, you'll find yourself either spending most of two days travelling, by taking a daytime ferry, or miss most of two nights' sleep by using a night ferry. And you can't pop over on impulse, except in the middle of winter, because you have to book the ferry crossing well in advance. Moreover, anyone who travels regularly knows that ferries can be delayed, and so can planes, if you are planning short breaks by air. French trains have an excellent record on timekeeping, but if you are calculating journey times, always allow plenty of time for connections.

Never forget, either, that long weekends are just the times when air traffic controllers or ferry operators are likely to go on strike, so as to inconvenience the maximum number of people. Many people, and not just out-and-out cynics, suspect that such considerations will also apply to the Channel Tunnel.

When you come to calculating driving times, again err on the side of caution. Side roads may not be as crowded as main roads, but you are more likely to get stuck behind a tractor or combine harvester, or, in the depths of the country, to be held up by a flock of sheep or goats. Winding country roads take time to negotiate, anyway, particularly if you are driving on the 'wrong' side of the road.

Take all these factors into account, and preferably travel to the area several times, at different times of day, before deciding that it really is accessible enough to be suitable for short breaks as well as a long summer holiday. Before buying a specific property in the countryside, again check how long it will take to get to the nearest shops, and to leisure facilities like swimming pools, or to the river for a bathe. Remember that you may be driving in the heat of the day – and that here, too, estate agents tend to be over-optimistic.

The Tunnel area

There are a number of misconceptions about northern France, with many buyers believing that Normandy starts at Calais. It doesn't, and the area close to the Channel Tunnel exit is part of the Nord-Pas-de-Calais region, also referred to by the old names of Artois and Picardie. The Channel Tunnel has made this area seem ideal for a weekend home for many buyers in southeast England, easier to get to than Devon and Cornwall, and offering the advantages of the French way of life on their doorstep. This was the boom area in the late eighties and is still quite popular. It is not the prettiest part of France and for many French people is associated with declining industries, but the river valleys of the Canche and Authie are attractive and there are some charming wooded areas with peaceful villages. The resort of Le Touquet with long sandy beaches and a well-known golf course has long been fashionable and a number of new coastal developments offer reasonably priced accommodation with no restoration problems. Many new roads are being built in this area and a second TGV line is also planned: check carefully before buying that they won't pass too close to your weekend retreat.

Climate
Much the same as southeast England.

Access
Once the Channel Tunnel is open, access should be excellent. Until then, you must use the curtailed ferry services operating from Calais to Dover and Ramsgate to Dunkirk (but no longer to Boulogne), the Seacats between Dover or Folkestone and Boulogne, or Dover and Calais, or the hovercraft between Dover and Calais.

Property and prices
Prices inevitably rose thanks to the British 'invasion', but they started from a low base as they had fallen in previous years due to industrial decline. There is little competition from the French in this area, except in the better-known seaside resorts, so there was never a truly dramatic rise, and prices dropped slightly after sterling's departure from the ERM put the brakes on British demand. Unconverted houses in the country, with water and electricity, start at about 200,000 francs. But you need to pay at least 450,000 francs to find a two- or three-bed cottage you can move straight into, according to Northern France Properties.* The demand for comfortable seaside flats has dwindled sharply and new developments are now few and far between.

General interest
Good beaches and sports opportunities and the closeness to Britain are the main attractions for most buyers, although the friendliness of the people, the 'military tourism' of the First World War battlefields, the interest of

towns like Saint-Omer, Montreuil, Arras and Amiens, and the vibrant cultural life of Lille deserve to be taken into account too. On the gastronomic front: good fresh seafood and Flemish-style braised beef with beer. Letting potential is quite good year-round to the British, but summer holidays further afield are usually preferred.

Further reading

Banker, Michael and Atterbury, Paul, *The North of France* (Heyford Press, 1990).

Bentley, James, *The Gateway to France, Flanders, Artois and Picardy* (Penguin, 1993).

Eperon, Barbara, *Normandy and Northern France* (Helm, 1991).

Regional tourist offices

44 Grand' Rue, 62200 Boulogne-sur-Mer; 21 rue Ernest-Cauvin, 80000 Amiens.

Normandy

Thanks to its relative proximity to Britain, its peaceful rolling countryside, its attractive half-timbered houses set in apple orchards, its old-established beach resorts like Deauville or Cabourg, plus perhaps a vague feeling of common ancestry derived from classroom memories of William the Conqueror, Normandy has long been a popular holiday destination for the British. It has increasingly become a holiday home area, too, as the Channel Tunnel and the motorway from Calais to Rouen (the Abbeville–Rouen stretch opened in 1993) make it more accessible.

Climate

Similar to southern England, especially by the coast; slightly warmer inland and noticeably wet round Rouen.

Access

The Channel ports of Caen, Dieppe and Le Havre are all in Normandy, but the crossings take several hours, which makes weekending difficult unless you are prepared to put up with two tiring overnight journeys. Beware estate agents' claims about speed of access from the Channel Tunnel (see page 22). At the moment it is still quite a slow drive from Calais to Rouen and beyond. The largely unspoilt Cotentin peninsula is easily reached from Cherbourg and the Mont Saint-Michel area from Saint-Malo, but again the crossings are long.

Airports to check out for current flights are Caen, Dinard, Le Havre and Rouen.

Rouen can be reached direct by train from Dieppe (1 hour) and Le Havre (1½ hours), Caen from Cherbourg (1½ hours), Alençon from Caen (1¼–1½ hours), or via Rouen from Dieppe or Le Havre.

Areas and prices

Vivian Bridge of Northern France Properties* says that 75 per cent of his clients want to be in the countryside or in a village, preferably in a pretty Norman-style half-timbered brick cottage or small house. The other 25 per cent want to be really close to the coast, a preference they share with French families. Resorts like Cabourg and Deauville have been chic for over a century: it has always been said that old money in France goes north, while the *nouveaux riches* go south to the Côte d'Azur. The picturesque little fishing town of Honfleur is very popular with weekending Parisians as well as with the British, while Ouistreham is a mecca for British yachtspeople. Dieppe had a large British colony in the nineteenth century and the region just inland is now popular for British weekend homes. The pretty Pays d'Auge south of Lisieux is also sought-after.

As in the Tunnel area, prices achieved dropped slightly after sterling left the ERM. Unmodernised Normandy-style houses in the countryside or in a village cost in the region of 200,000 to 250,000 francs and would need at least another 200,000 francs spent on them. For 400,000 francs you can find a two- or three-bedroomed cottage ready to move into (though not necessarily done up to British standards of comfort), with a modernised kitchen, some traditional features, a pleasant outlook, probably an outbuilding or two, and about ¾ acre of land, according to Northern France Properties.

General interest

Normandy has many places of interest – attractively restored Rouen, Bayeux and its Tapestry, Caen, with twin abbeys and William the Conqueror's castle, and the Mont Saint-Michel. You can visit the D-Day landing beaches and explore the abbeys in the Seine Valley. There is good riding, walking and angling in the inland areas and water sports of all kinds on the coast. Norman cuisine is an added attraction: dishes based on the rich butter and cream produced on the lush pastureland, with cider and *calvados* ingredients in many sauces. Duck dishes are famous in the Rouen area and sole and mussels on the coast. Pont l'Evêque and Camembert are just two of the cheeses for which Normandy is well known and 'Norman apple tart' is a byword for juicy, tasty apples in crisp pastry.

The popularity of the region with both the French and the British means that letting should not be a problem.

Further reading

Eperon, Barbara, *Normandy and Northern France* (Helm, 1991).
McNeill, John, *Blue Guide Normandy* (A & C Black, 1993).
Naylor, Kim, *Discover Normandy* (Berlitz, 1992).
Roberts, Nesta, *Companion Guide to Normandy* (Collins, 1986).

Regional tourist offices

35 rue Joséphine, 27000 Evreux; 25 pl. de la Cathédrale, 76008 Rouen.

Brittany

The jagged windswept region jutting out into the sea on France's north-western tip, which has many affinities with Cornwall (not least its Celtic heritage), is a favourite family holiday area for both the French and the British. With its long coastline – over a thousand kilometres of granite headlands, tiny coves, sandy beaches, picturesque fishing harbours – and its green and peaceful inland regions, it is very varied yet largely unspoilt, and is known for its low prices and proudly independent people.

Access

Easily reached from the west of England if you don't mind the long ferry crossings from Portsmouth, Plymouth and Southampton to Saint-Malo and Roscoff, and from the Channel Islands by ferry, catamaran or hydro-foil. It's a good eight hours' drive from the eastern Channel ports to Brittany's eastern border, at least ten hours to the southern coast.

Check out flights to Brest, Nantes, Quimper and Rennes. The arrival of the TGV in western France has slashed rail journeys to Brittany from Paris: Paris–Rennes 2 hours, Paris-Brest 4 hours. To Quimper: 5¼ hours changing from TGV at Rennes or Brest, 6½ hours direct.

Climate

Similar to southwest England in most places, with rain quite common in summer and windy beaches in the north and west; the south enjoys a very mild micro-climate (even mimosa grows there).

Areas and prices

Granite houses with slate roofs can be found all over Brittany, the majority in need of substantial renovation. Prices are generally a little lower than in the sunnier southwest, starting at about 200,000 francs for basic rural dwellings, although the number of very cheap places is dwindling as Brittany becomes increasingly popular with British buyers. Two- or three-bedroomed houses in reasonable condition start at about 350,000 francs and larger houses with some land at about 500,000 francs. Manor houses and priories and the like can occasionally be found, starting at about 800,000 francs in good condition with a fair amount of land. In the south are a number of new developments where flats and small villas or semi-detached houses can be bought: a modern two-bedroomed house here would start at about 450,000 francs, say Barbers.*

General interest

A region with its own personality and much of interest to offer, with its varied scenery, good sports opportunities and interesting history and customs (local costume is still often worn and religious and other festivals take place throughout the year). Interesting architecture (old stone calvaries, attractive stone-built towns, the Mont Saint-Michel, and famous prehistoric cromlechs and standing stones). Excellent fish and shellfish at much lower prices than on the Mediterranean, pancakes and cider a universal speciality, succulent lamb from the salt marshes near the coast.

Letting potential is good, with British families in country properties, and both French and British on the coast.

Further reading
Dawes, Frank Victor, *Brittany* (Helm, 1989).
Insight Guide to Brittany (Geo UK, 1989).
Spence, Keith, *Brittany* (George Philip, 1992).

Regional tourist office
Pont de Nemours, 35025 Rennes cédex.

The Touraine

This central portion of the Loire Valley is a lush agricultural area criss-crossed by rivers, flat but very pleasant. A region of orchards, market gardens and vineyards, it is also a major tourist area thanks to the famous Loire Valley châteaux. Yet even at the height of the season it remains peaceful, with all but the roads leading to the major châteaux virtually empty. As well as attractive and quite lively Tours, there are a number of pleasant small towns, some with medieval centres.

Climate
Mild, damp winters and very hot and sunny but sometimes unpleasantly humid summers. A good area for gardeners, but if you're planning a holiday home, you'll need to find someone to keep the garden under control – or else buy a scythe!

Access
From Calais or Boulogne via Paris (A10 motorway to Blois or Tours), from Le Havre via Lisieux and Alençon, from Dieppe via Rouen and Chartres or Alençon, from Caen via Alençon. Look into direct flights to Tours (generally only in summer months). The new TGV to the west coast means that Saint-Pierre-des-Corps, a suburb of Tours, is only an hour's journey from Paris; a five-minute shuttle service runs into the centre. To avoid Paris you can fly from Gatwick to Caen, followed by a pretty three-hour train ride.

Types of property and prices
A major building material is tufa, a crumbly limestone that becomes whiter with age. As well as the usual range of rural stone buildings, you may find a one-room shelter for temporary labour during the grape harvest, known as a *loge de vigne*. A prosperous region for centuries, it has many substantial houses and a good choice of manor houses and châteaux from all periods. Roofs are generally of slate, occasionally of flat tiles.

As the Touraine has long been popular with the French for weekend houses, a large amount of property has already been restored, although you can still find *fermettes* and barns for conversion (about 200,000 francs if total restoration is needed, 350,000 to 450,000 francs if structurally sound and a reasonable size). Already converted they cost up to about 600,000 francs. Manor houses with some land will certainly be over one million francs, twice as much if fully modernised, and the sought-after châteaux start around two million francs and can go right up to twenty million.

As the arrival of the TGV was soon followed by the beginning of the recession in France, it did not have as big an effect on property prices as anticipated. However people working in Paris are starting to commute from the Touraine, and town houses have risen slightly. Country properties do not seem to have been affected.

General interest
As well as the châteaux and the attractive towns, this is a good area for anglers and for riding, and for gourmets. *Charcuterie*, freshwater fish in wine-based sauces, dishes with prunes and goat's milk cheeses are the main culinary specialities, while popular local wines include the grapey Touraine Sauvignon, sparkling Saumur champenoise, and two well-known reds, Chinon and Bourgueil.

With all these plus points, it should be reasonably easy to let to French or foreign holidaymakers.

Further reading
Binny, Marcus, *Châteaux of the Loire* (Penguin, 1992).
Eperon, Arthur and Barbara, *The Loire Valley* (Helm, 1989).
Insight Guide to the Loire Valley (Geo UK, 1991).

Regional tourist offices
10 rue du Colombier, BP 2412, 45000 Orléans; 16 rue de Buffon, 37032 Tours.

The two Charentes
After a rush of British buyers in the North in 1988 and in Normandy in 1989, the early nineties saw a boom in the Charente and Charente-Maritime. Second-home seekers who find the Dordogne, to the south, too crowded with their compatriots and/or too expensive started venturing into this unspoilt region of western France that has been opened up to an extent by the arrival of the Atlantic line of the high-speed train service. The coastal region has been slowly developed in recent years, with marinas and golf courses and holiday villages springing up and plenty of water sports facilities. But it has not been overdeveloped and the sea is generally clear and clean – and also cold for much of the year. The inland region is watered by the river Charente, close to which the vines that produce the cognac grapes have been grown for centuries. Not as pretty as the Dordogne, but the region has great charm and the lowish prices are an added attraction.

Climate

Long sunny summers, without the very high coastal temperatures on the Mediterranean. Mostly wet springs and mild winters, although coastal areas can be stormy.

Access

From Calais and Boulogne via Rouen and Le Mans to Tours, where you join the A10 motorway, or via Paris and again the A10. From the Normandy ports via Alençon to Le Mans first. From the Brittany ports via Rennes and Nantes to La Rochelle or Poitiers. Motorail service Calais–Bordeaux.

Convenient major airports are Bordeaux and Nantes; look into Poitiers and Angoulême too. TGV service to the Atlantic has cut rail time to Poitiers to about 1½ hours, to Angoulême to under 2½ hours, to Bordeaux to 3 hours, Niort (under 2½ hours) and La Rochelle (3 hours).

Types of property and prices

The typical Charentaise house is long, low and stone-built and set in a walled courtyard. The usual range of rural properties can be found inland at lower prices generally than in the Dordogne; as the pool of such places shows no sign of drying up, the recent boom did not have a dramatic effect on prices. Spratley & Co* speak of them as the most reasonable in the southwest, only about a third of British prices for comparable village houses. The Charente Maritime is a different market, they say, with modern houses and flats also available on the coast, at prices ranging from about 450,000 francs upwards.

General interest

Good beaches for family holidays, plenty of sports opportunities both on the coast and inland (riding and angling), some attractive fishing ports, the Old Town of La Rochelle and its good New World Museum and, inland from the town, the curious Marais Poitevin, a fenland region crisscrossed by canals, now a nature reserve. Cognac is an attractive small town and Saintes, with Roman remains, and Angoulême's elaborate Romanesque cathedral are all worth exploring. Excellent oysters on the coast, cognac-based sauces and good *charcuterie* inland.

Regional tourist offices

11bis rue des Augustins, BP 1152, 17008 La Rochelle cédex, 18 rue du Rempart, 79000 Niort.

The Dordogne and the Lot

The Dordogne has been popular with the British for permanent homes in retirement and for second homes for several decades, no doubt because both the climate and the rolling green landscape dotted with stone houses are somewhat reminiscent of the prettier country areas of England such as the Cotswolds. If you are looking for a French home in a region with a flourishing British community, this must be a good choice.

The Lot is wilder and generally drier and hotter, a poor rural area ideal for getting away from urban bustle. Popular for some time with British artists and writers seeking quiet and beautiful surroundings, it has also attracted a number of second-home buyers.

Climate
Temperate in the Dordogne, with a fair amount of rainfall, so good for gardening. Hotter summers and less rainfall in the Lot: not a place for well-stocked flower gardens, though roses and peonies do well.

Access
The fastest way from the eastern Channel ports is via Paris and the A10 motorway, or you could try the A71 from Orléans via Montluçon; from the Normandy ports via Alençon, Le Mans and Tours, from the Brittany ports via Rennes, Nantes and Saintes. Motorail from Calais to Brive, Bordeaux and Toulouse.

Major airports are Bordeaux and Toulouse, but Brive also offers possibilities. Fast trains from Paris to Brive (4¼ hours) and Cahors (5½ hours), via Limoges to Périgueux (5 hours).

Property and prices
In the north of the region the typical building is the *maison périgourdine*, a long, low structure with a steeply pitched roof made of flat tiles; further south the *maison quercynoise*, though usually smaller, often has two storeys and a shallower roof of rounded tiles, with loft space. A much sought-after feature, though found on fewer than one in fifty buildings according to local agents, is the *pigeonnier*, a dovecot attached to the house in the form of a square (or sometimes rectangular) tower. Modest rural buildings may have a *souillarde* or *évier quercynois*, a stone sink set into the wall, often with quite an elaborate archway above it.

Prices are generally a little lower in the Lot, whose popularity is more recent. They did go up slightly as a result of British buyers becoming active there, but from a low base in what is basically a poor area with few elaborate buildings. Small unconverted cottages and barns can still be found for 150,000 francs upwards, though their numbers are dwindling – and they will, of course, need at least another 500,000 francs spent on them to make them halfway comfortable. Prices for two- or three-bedroomed houses in the country needing complete or partial restoration start in this part of France at about 350,000 francs, rising to 600,000 francs. Converted and restored they fetch about 600,000 to 800,000 francs. More substantial houses with restored outbuildings joined to the main building start at about 1 million francs. Châteaux and other grand houses range in price from 2½ million to 20 million francs.

General interest
Not an area of major tourist sights, but many interesting and attractive old towns and villages (some, like Sarlat, superbly restored) and the famous prehistoric caves round Les Eyzies-de-Tayac. This part of France is also well-known for its cuisine, replete with truffles and *foie gras*, and rich goose and duck dishes. Cahors and Bergerac, though not in the same class as the clarets produced nearby, are both good red wines, drunk throughout France. The popularity of the region with the British means that letting potential is good, and many other nations favour the Dordogne too.

Further reading
Barber, Richard, *Companion Guide to Gascony and the Dordogne* (Collins, 1991).
Eperon, Arthur and Barbara, *The Dordogne and Lot* (Helm, 1989).
White, Freda, *Three Rivers of France* (Faber, 1991).

Regional tourist offices
16 rue du Président-Wilson, 24000 Périgueux; Chambre de Commerce, 46000 Cahors.

Languedoc and Roussillon
The coastal area of these two ancient provinces, now combined to form a single economic region, stretches from the Pyrenees on the Spanish border to the western edge of Provence near the Rhône delta. It has witnessed large-scale development since a plan was drawn up in the sixties to conjure up a second Riviera by dredging the mosquito-infested lagoons and building a string of new resorts with enough facilities to attract an international clientele, yet budget-priced enough to stem the growing tide of French families heading for Spain for their holidays. Inland, the countryside seems to have changed little for centuries, with sleepy villages, old stone farmhouses and ruined Cathar castles. Vineyards, too, stretching as far as the eye can see, although the wine is by no means France's best and some of the land under vines is being turned back to other crops as Europe's wine lake expands inexorably. In the Pyrenees above Perpignan are several sunny ski resorts, some of them also popular for summer holidays.

Climate
Very hot and sunny summers, relatively cold winters bedevilled by the strong *tramontane* wind. Even in summer the resorts at the southern end can be unpleasantly windy.

Access
The classic (and long) road route from Calais or Boulogne is the A1 to Paris, then the A6/7 to Avignon and the A9 to Montpellier, Béziers, Narbonne and Perpignan. From the western Channel ports you can drive south to Tours, then take the much less congested A10 to Bordeaux and

the A61 to Narbonne. You can avoid a lot of tiring driving by using the Motorail service from Calais to Narbonne.

The main international airport is Montpellier, but Perpignan can also prove useful. Many British owners now prefer to fly to Barcelona, taking advantage of cheaper flights and much cheaper car hire than in France. Thanks to the TGV, Paris to Montpellier takes under 5 hours, Paris to Béziers about 5½ hours. You can save time by travelling overnight from Paris to Agde, Béziers, Montpellier, Narbonne, Perpignan or Sète.

Types of property and prices

Flats in new developments in the sunny coastal resorts are popular with many northern Europeans. Propriétés Roussillon* speak of small studio flats in the southerly resorts, with balcony, kitchenette and shower room, from 160,000 francs, up to luxury five-bedroomed flats, fully furnished, with parking space and basement storage space area, close to 1.3 million francs. A luxury flat near the golf course in Saint-Cyprien would be considerably more. Exclusive Port-Camargue, popular with yachtsmen, is also expensive. Flats and chalets in the ski resorts are also available. But here you now face competition from the Spaniards, who have been buying heavily in Les Angles and Font-Romeu. As a result, a modern centrally-heated chalet in an all-year resort like Les Angles, with three bedrooms, two bathrooms and two balconies, now costs 650,000 francs, say the same agency.

Inland, you can find small stone houses to renovate in the picturesque hill villages for under 200,000 francs. Most villages have mains water and drainage, but at this price they will need total rewiring and replumbing as well as extensive restoration. A renovated village house with two or three bedrooms, terrace and garden would cost around 400,000–500,000 francs. The region has a number of large *mas* or farmhouses, with outbuildings. Modernised they cost in the region of 1.5 million francs.

Montpellier, an attractive university town that has recently become a major commercial centre, has a number of modern housing developments, and the occasional flat in the elegant old town houses in the centre.

General interest

The modern coastal resorts are well-equipped, and popular with children for their sandy beaches and water sports amenities, but are not to everyone's taste with their futuristic architecture and their general lack of pleasant little restaurants. But there are attractive small fishing harbours nearby, like Sète or Palavas, and you can escape from the busy coast into the peaceful hinterland to visit the fortress of Carcassonne and Fontfroide Abbey, the Cathar castles and the wild upland reaches of the Cévennes with their nature reserve.

The cuisine on the coast is based on excellent Mediterranean fish and shellfish, often in pungent garlicky sauces, plus the oysters for which this area is famous. As you approach Perpignan it takes on a pronounced Spanish flavour. Inland the most famous dish is *cassoulet*, a filling bean and lamb stew, but the Cévennes area has many interesting dishes using local mushrooms and tasty lamb and delicious goat's milk cheeses. The wines of the area are mostly rather thin, though *clairette* and the sparkling *blanquette de Limoux* can be good. In Roussillon the natural sweet wines known as Rivesaltes and Banyuls are popular apéritifs.

There should be little difficulty in letting in the summer months, to British, French or other northern European holidaymakers, but the windy winter climate does not favour year-round letting.

Further reading
Bentley, James, *Languedoc* (George Philip, 1987).
Eperon, Arthur, *Lot (Quercy)* (Pan 1990).
Law, Joy, *The Midi* (John Murray, 1991).
Sanger, Andrew, *Languedoc and Roussillon* (Helm, 1989).

Regional tourist office
12 rue Foch, 34000 Montpellier.

The Côte d'Azur
Still better known to the British as the French Riviera, the Côte d'Azur is the archetypal 'South of France', with all that that implies in the way of wealth and luxury. The narrow coastal strip stretching beside the Mediterranean from the Italian border at Menton westwards to Cannes has been popular with the well-heeled British since the nineteenth century and this western end is still the most expensive, with villas costing tens of millions of francs on the sought-after peninsulas like Cap Ferrat and Cap d'Antibes. The Côte is now deemed to expand westwards to chic Saint-Tropez and on to the more popular resorts between there and Toulon, which are very crowded throughout the summer season with holiday-makers from all over Europe.

Climate
Mainly mild winters and hot dry summers, with rainfall generally restricted to the spring. Winds can be strong and make gardening a problem, especially in exposed areas, as well as causing forest fires in summer. Watering, too, is a major problem for second-home owners.

Access
A long drive from the Channel ports (A6/7 from Paris to near Marseille, then A8 eastwards to Cannes and various coast roads) can be avoided by the Motorail service from Calais to Fréjus/Saint Raphaël or Nice. Flights to Nice and Marseille.

Overnight rail journeys from Calais and Paris to Nice and on to Menton and the Italian resorts; in the daytime, TGV from Paris takes 5¼ hours to Toulon and 7 hours to Nice (the Nice run will be cut to 4 hours by the end of the century).

Property and prices

Although this is mainly an area for the very rich, you can find some reasonably priced flats a little bit away from the sea, behind Antibes, for instance, or in new developments in Cannes, Nice or Grasse. Studio flats in, say, Fréjus start at about 450,000 francs. Generally speaking, the western resorts are less expensive than the eastern, but anywhere near a golf course will always be expensive.

General interest

Holiday country *par excellence*, with the usual Mediterranean plus points and plenty of culture, too, including excellent modern art museums. Garlicky Mediterranean cuisine based on fish, good vegetable dishes in the Italianate Nice repertoire. This area is so sought after year-round that letting should be no problem.

Further reading

Facaros, Dana and Pauls, Michael, *The South of France* (Cadogan, 1992).
Jacobs, Michael, *A Guide to Provence* (Penguin, 1989).
Lyall, Archibald, *Companion Guide to the South of France* (Collins, 1990).
Macdonald, Roger, *Provence and the Côte d'Azur* (Helm, 1989).

Regional tourist office

av. Thiers, 06000 Nice.

Other areas that appeal to the British

There are some other parts of France that are not particularly in demand at the moment, but that have attracted considerable numbers of British second-home owners in earlier periods, before the late eighties boom got under way. They could be described as connoisseurs' regions, appealing to long-term Francophiles.

The Ardèche

This is a fairly wild and poor rural area, on the southeastern edge of the Massif Central. Arid in the south, where the Gorges de l'Ardèche attract vast numbers of campers and holidaymakers in the summer, it is greener in the north, with chestnut forests and an upland area culminating in the Mont Gerbier de Jonc, a curious outcrop of black volcanic rock at the foot of which spurts the source of the River Loire. Aubenas, Largentière and Vals-les-Bains are all attractive small towns, but there are no major tourist sights.

The Ardèche has been popular with the Dutch for many years and, to a lesser extent, with the British. It also became a favourite retreat for the French intellectuals who dropped out after the 1968 'revolution' and turned to making goat's milk cheese in isolated farmhouses or weaving and potting. The area has a strong tradition of local craftsmanship and an interesting rustic cuisine with a good range of *charcuterie* and many dishes based on or garnished with the chestnuts that grow there in profusion.

Access

A1 motorway to Paris, then A6/A7 to Loriol or Montélimar, or Motorail service from Calais or Dieppe to Avignon; flights to Lyon or (via Paris) to Avignon; train to Montélimar (some TGVs stop there) or, a very beautiful but slow route, on the Cévenol train to La Bastide-Saint-Laurent.

Property and prices

As well as the usual range of rural buildings, usually uninhabited for many years, the Ardèche has the occasional *magnanerie* or silkworm farm (the region was once full of the mulberry trees on which silkworms feed). Prices are generally lower than in more sought-after areas.

Further reading

Stevenson, Robert Louis, *Travels with a Donkey* (Chatto & Windus, 1986; illustrated with photographs and paintings of the region).
White, Freda, *West of the Rhône* (Faber, 1964).
The Visitor's Guide to the Massif Central (Moorland, 1989).

Burgundy

A rich agricultural area famous for its wines, its historic towns (Beaune, Dijon), its important buildings (the Romanesque basilica at Vézelay, Tournus and its Romanesque abbey, the Gothic cathedral of Sens, the abbey of Fontenay) and its excellent cuisine, based on meat and fish in rich sauces. Canal-boat holidays with gourmet cuisine have long been popular with the British.

Climate

Long hot summers, damp and often foggy winters.

Access

To Paris via A1 motorway from the eastern Channel ports, the A13 from the Norman gateways, then A6 to Burgundy (branch off at Pouilly-en-Auxois for Dijon). Flights to Dijon, or Lyon for southern Burgundy. TGV rail service Paris–Dijon in about 1½ hours, Paris–Mâcon 1¾ hours.

Property and prices

While northern Burgundy, popular with Parisians for weekend homes, is quite expensive, the south is still relatively undiscovered, say Barbers,* who can suggest a good choice of quite cheap houses near Mâcon and Cluny, some with a covered verandah known as a *galerie Maconnaise*. Houses of this type, needing finishing, cost from about 350,000 francs. When renovated, they will sell for 600,000 upwards.

Further reading
Speaight, Robert (revised Francis Pagan), *Companion Guide to Burgundy* (Collins, 1990).
Dunlop, Ian, *Burgundy* (Hamish Hamilton, 1990).
Ousby, Ian, *Blue Guide Burgundy* (A & C Black, 1992).

Regional tourist office
55 rue de la Préfecture, 21041 Dijon.

Provence

Long popular with discerning Francophiles for its rambling old villas and low farmhouses surrounded by lavender-covered hills, Provence is still delightful (despite the hype resulting from an influx of Peter Mayle fans), but such places are now rarely available unconverted and fetch high prices when converted. Moreover, relocation and decentralisation by French companies, and by multinational companies for their French headquarters, especially in the advanced technology sectors, means that top executives with high salaries have bought in the area, pushing up prices both for the few old farmhouses left and for modern villas. The Lubéron has also become something of an international jet-set holiday rendezvous.

Climate
Hot dry summers, wet springs, sometimes quite cold winters, bedevilled at all times by the *mistral* wind.

Access
As for the Côte d'Azur. The TGV from Paris reaches Avignon in under 4 hours, Nîmes in 4¼ hours. Motorail from Calais and Dieppe to Avignon.

Property and prices
You can occasionally find village houses ranging upwards from 500,000 francs. Modern villas start at about 800,000 francs and can go up to several million. A largish restored *mas*, the typical low Provençal farmhouse with shallow tiled roof, starts at about 1.5 million francs.

Further reading
Jacobs, Michael, *A Guide to Provence* (Penguin, 1989).
Macdonald, Roger, *Provence and the Côte d'Azur* (Helm, 1989).
Lyall, Archibald, *Companion Guide to the South of France* (Collins, 1990).
Mayle, Peter, *A Year in Provence* (Pan, 1990); *Toujours Provence* (Pan, 1992).

Regional tourist office
41 cours Jean-Jaurès, 84000 Avignon.

Also worth a look

Finally, brief details of some regions that have so far attracted relatively few British property buyers but are certainly worth exploring.

Alsace has failed to feature to any appreciable degree in the market as yet. Distance from the sea and severe winter weather (summers are hot and sunny) are no doubt two reasons for this. Another must be the curious fact that many British people are not aware that this eastern region is in France. Yet another is that there is relatively little property to renovate. Alsace is the smallest of France's economic regions, and a mainly prosperous one. It has not seen the same massive rural exodus that has emptied farms and cottages in poorer areas. This, plus a long-standing tradition of maintaining houses and villages in spick-and-span condition, means that tumbledown dwellings ripe for modernisation are few and far between.

But for those who worry about getting bored with holidaying in the same place every year, this very attractive region has much to offer: it is within a short drive of West Germany and Switzerland, and not far from Luxembourg, so that you can combine your French holiday with, say, excursions into the Black Forest or the Swiss lakes. And Alsace itself is full of interest, historically, culturally and gastronomically, with major museums in Colmar and Strasbourg, dozens of picturesque villages on the Wine Road, cross-country skiing in the mountains, delicious fruity wines and more Michelin restaurant stars than any other French region. Communications are good, too. The A26 from Calais joins the A4 to Strasbourg at Rheims; there is a direct train service from Calais (about 6½ hours to Strasbourg), and flights from London to Strasbourg and Mulhouse/Basel.

Because of the regular influx of Eurocrats and the importance of Strasbourg as a business and financial centre, property prices are not cheap. And now that it has been decided that the European Parliament will continue to hold sessions there, they are likely to remain fairly high compared to some other regions. As the Single European Market puts the emphasis on business exchanges between the EC countries, Alsace is well placed to benefit from this cross-border boom and in the long term prices are likely to go up.

The **Berry**, a peaceful region right in the centre of France, is well off the beaten tourist track – Bourges must be the least visited of the great French cathedrals – but does not deserve this neglect. A mainly rural area, where centuries-old traditions have survived – sorcery is still said to be rife – it has a number of attractive châteaux and villages. It is only a short drive into the hunting-shooting-and-fishing paradise of the Sologne, a mysterious land of meres and thick woods, and to the great Loire Valley châteaux. Burgundy and the Auvergne are both quite near too.

As there is no motorway from Paris prices have not generally been pushed up by Parisians buying weekend cottages. But the journey from Britain is fairly painless: the drive from Dieppe or Le Havre via Rouen,

Chartres and Orléans offers plenty of interest. Direct trains from Paris in about 1½ hours.

The **Drôme**, on the other side of the A7 motorway from the Ardèche, does not seem to have enjoyed the same popularity. A lavender-filled rural area with a dry climate (the lowest rainfall figures in France), it is easily reached by motorway to Loriol or Montélimar, by plane to Lyon or by TGV to Montélimar. It is well placed for excursions into the Lower Alps and into Provence, and has some attractive places of its own – the little town of Crest, the château of Grignan, where the Marquise de Sévigné wrote many of her letters, medieval Nyons, Dieulefit, a crafts centre, all reached by delightfully traffic-free roads.

Gascony, and the *département* of the Gers at its heart, is a hilly rural region, warm and sunny for most of the year, but with a climate influenced by the fresher air blown in from the Atlantic. It is within easy reach of the Pyrenees and famous for its rich cuisine and its armagnacs, yet is still relatively undiscovered by foreign tourists and home-buyers. It is a good area for houses of character, says Ian Purslow,* both in its *bastides* or medieval fortified towns and in the countryside, where you can find handsome *maisons de maître* (see Chapter 4), many of them eighteenth-century, as well as farmhouses and cottages. Access is good: frequent flights to Toulouse and Tarbes – and Bordeaux isn't far either; the TGV Atlantique stops at Agen, Tarbes and Toulouse, and the region is well served by motorways.

The rolling countryside of the **Limousin**, on the northwestern edge of the Massif Central, is largely unspoilt, and tends to be ignored by British holidaymakers and househunters travelling through or past it to the Charente and the Dordogne. A farming area with good angling and riding, and an interesting small capital in the porcelain centre of Limoges, it is worth considering for those who like peace and quiet and has recently attracted interest from those who find areas like the Dordogne too crowded with the British for comfort. Prices are reasonably low and the range of property is good, from cottages and farm buildings to manor houses and châteaux.

Access from Boulogne or Calais via Paris, the A10 motorway to Poitiers, then the N147 to Limoges; or leave the motorway at Blois and cut across country. A third alternative is to drive via the motorway to Montluçon. From the western ports, proceed via Le Mans and Tours. The Motorail service to Brive saves driving time. Limoges is on the main rail line to Toulouse (about 3¼ hours from Paris) and there are several flights a day from Paris. You can also fly to Bordeaux or Brive.

Also starting to attract interest from those who want to branch out from the better-known regions are the **Lozère** and the **Aveyron**, sparsely populated mountainous *départements* on the fringe of the popular south-west. The Lozère is on the tourist map because of the spectacular Gorges du Tarn but the Aveyron, between the Lot and the Tarn, is little known outside France. It has some medieval walled villages, the limestone caves where Roquefort ewe's milk cheese is ripened, a surprisingly lively capital in Rodez and some pretty villages. Both here and in the more austere Lozère you can find small stone cottages and farmhouses at low prices. But Madeleine Vallet at Lesenéchal Immobilier* also speaks of more spacious converted farmhouses with lovely views, and watermills beside the Aveyron.

The climate here is quite harsh: very hot in summer and bleak in winter. And it's a long drive from Clermont-Ferrand through the Massif Central. But for lovers of solitude and natural grandeur, for those who want to be genuinely miles from anywhere, this area is certainly worth looking at. You can fly to Montpellier, or travel there by TGV, then continue by train to Mende; there is a rail service between Brive (on the fast main line to Toulouse) and Rodez; or you can take the Motorail service from Calais to Brive. Flights from Paris to Mende and to Rodez are also useful.

Buying in Paris

Increasing interest is being shown in Paris by British buyers, despite the fact that it is one of the world's most expensive cities in terms of property prices. However there has been a marked fall in prices recently, assessed by some experts as amounting to as much as a third overall. Letting potential in the city, including short-term furnished lets, is excellent, as there remains a shortage of accommodation.

Prices naturally vary from one district to another, with parts of the fifth, and the sixth and seventh *arrondissements* on the Left Bank, and the fourth, eighth and sixteenth on the Right Bank traditionally the most sought-after. Prices achieved in the last quarter of 1992 showed the following averages per square metre: 25,700 francs in the fourth (the Marais), 24,700 francs in the fifth (Latin Quarter), 26,700 francs in the sixth (Saint-Germain-des-Près), 32,000 in the eighth. However you should bear in mind that even the posh eighth *arrondissement* (which includes the Champs-Elysées) also covers a somewhat seedy area round Saint-Lazare station, which brings the average down; this means that prices in the top streets work out considerably higher.

Garages or parking spaces in underground carparks below blocks of flats are a much sought-after commodity. In districts like the fifth or sixth *arrondissements*, where narrow streets and traffic congestion make street parking very difficult, garages cost a good 250,000 francs to buy. If you bought somewhere for your own use with a garage, but did not want to drive in Paris, you could let it out in some areas for at least 1000 francs a month.

It is important to be aware that flats in Paris (and the very few houses available) are liable to be in poor condition as regards wiring and plumbing. This often applies even to modern property. The French are curiously undemanding about such matters – try to buy somewhere that has been done up by a foreigner! In particular, beware of places with electric convector heaters fixed to the walls. They are very expensive to run, are liable to overload the system even if you are paying for a high power standing charge, and often do not provide satisfactory heating in Paris's damp winter climate, particularly in a large room, though they do have the advantage of heating up quickly if you will be making a lot of short trips to your Paris base. Moreover, many people find the very dry heat they produce trying. Unfortunately many old buildings renovated in the eighties and early nineties do have just such heating (there may well be no gas pipes in the whole block or group of blocks). But the government, which pushed electric heating furiously for many years, is now having second thoughts, and developers are being encouraged to install full central heating fired by gas or oil, or what is known as *chauffage urbain* (fired by steam from urban refuse).

If you yearn for the *vie de château* but don't feel like being stuck out in the country, you could acquire a flat in one of the aristocratic town houses that once filled districts like the Marais. Philip Hawkes* have a number of flats in historic buildings in Paris, some with magnificent painted ceilings, but prices are of course very high indeed.

An interesting fact: it is generally reckoned that about 50 per cent of Paris flats change hands privately, rather than through an estate agent.

Testing out your choice

Once you have selected the region that seems right for you and have visited it thoroughly to confirm your impression, the best way to make sure that it suits your purposes is to use the *gîte* system to rent something first – a cottage or farmhouse or a wing of a château, depending on what type of property you're thinking of buying. Preferably stay there several times, at different times of year, to see what problems and snags you may encounter, to make sure you like the climate, to check out transport and amenities. Don't be rushed. Always remember that prices in provincial France have never escalated as they have in boom periods in Britain.

Another advantage of this testing-out process is that you'll get to know some local people and will therefore have some ready-made contacts when you come back as househunters and, later on, when you need advice on builders or plumbers or gardeners. And by being really familiar with the area, and the type of property available, you're very unlikely to rush into buying the wrong place, which is only too easy if you haven't done the spade work first.

3 BUYING YOUR HOME

Before you start looking seriously for a house or flat, you should familiarise yourself with the conveyancing process in France. It is different in many respects from the method you are used to at home and you will feel much more comfortable if you know what will happen once you have found the right place.

First, two important facts. One is that all property in France is freehold, so the system of buying, say, a ninety-nine year lease does not exist. Second, the French equivalent of the Land Registry, known as the *cadastre* and originally set up by Napoleon, maintains plans in its local offices showing all land divided up into lots or parcels (*parcelles*), each with its own number and an indication of its use (residential, agricultural, industrial etc.). The *cadastre* operates in conjunction with the local *bureau des hypothèques*, which keeps a register of mortgages and charges affecting the title to the land, and records all transfers of land. Proof of ownership of a property is the fact that its sale to you has been registered in this way, rather than a bundle of title deeds.

Intermediaries

The first step must be to agree the price with the vendor and/or the intermediary negotiating the sale, who will be either an estate agent (*agent immobilier*) or a *notaire*, the lawyer who also handles the conveyancing of property in France.

Estate agents

French estate agents have to be licensed by the local authorities and must display prominently in their premises their official numbered certificate or licence (*carte de transactions sur immeubles*), which is renewable annually. They are also required by law to have insurance cover for professional negligence and to be covered by a financial guarantee. The guarantee figure must again be displayed. If it is over 500,000 francs, they are entitled to handle clients' deposits.

It is sensible to make your first appointment with agents at their premises, so that you can check their credentials by looking for the licence on the wall. It is unlikely that any agent you are put in touch with via a British agent will prove to be a cowboy, but it is better to be safe than sorry.

Most reputable agents are members of the estate agents' association, the Fédération nationale des agents immobiliers: look for the letters FNAIM on their premises and their letterhead.

Estate agents must have a written authority (*un mandat*) from sellers stating that they are authorised to negotiate on their behalf, but it is worth remembering that sole agencies are rare in France. They are empowered to draw up preliminary agreements, the first stage in the conveyancing process, and, provided they have the necessary financial guarantee, to take the deposit due from the buyer when this preliminary contract is signed.

Who pays the commission?

Most experts will tell you that it is generally the seller who pays the agent's commission these days, but that there may be regional variations. In practice, the seller certainly pays in the south and in Paris. This is also normally the case in Normandy. But in the Touraine and in the southwest (the Dordogne and the Lot, where many British people buy) and in Alsace, the buyer normally pays. Elsewhere it may be one or the other. And anywhere except Paris and the south, the commission may be split between buyer and seller.

If you query this variation with a French agent or *notaire*, the stock answer, accompanied by a Gallic shrug, is that it doesn't make any difference: if the vendor has to pay, he will simply add the commission on to what he believes to be the right asking price. So as the buyer you will be paying either way.

They have a point of course. But what interests you is knowing exactly how much money you are going to have to produce in the end. So do make absolutely certain that you know whether or not the price you have been quoted includes the agent's commission, or whether you will be having to pay it on top.

An increasing number of agents, particularly in Britain, now quote all-inclusive prices in their advertisements. But again, make absolutely sure whether this includes just the agent's commission, or the commission plus the *notaire*'s fee and the various taxes he is obliged to levy on the transaction. In theory property advertisements in France are supposed now to include the agent's commission. But this does not always happen in practice. And when you are discussing a deal with an agent, he or she may well be speaking in terms of the figure that will actually go to the seller, sometimes referred to as the *prix net vendeur*.

Once again there is no substitute for asking the agent or notaire, and make sure that it is put in writing.

How much is the commission?

Estate agent's commissions are much higher than in Britain. They are usually worked out on a sliding scale depending on the selling price, but they are no longer regulated by law. In practice, for the sake of simplicity, most agents stick to figures very close to the old official *barême* or scale of fees. And you are likely to find all agents within one town or region applying the same percentages.

Agents with many foreign clients often have their scale of fees pinned up on a wall. A typical chart in southwest France will look something like this:

100,000 frs	10%
200,000 frs	9%
300,000 frs	8%
400,000 frs	7%
500,000 frs	6.5%
600,000 frs	6%
700,000 frs	5.5%
800,000 frs upwards	5%

But once again, you must check the exact figure with the agent.

Notaires

Fees and taxes paid to *notaires* are always the responsibility of the buyer. It is important to understand the role played by *notaires* in the buying and selling of property. To do so, you must start by forgetting everything you know about the role played by solicitors in property transactions in England and Wales (the Scottish system is not quite the same). You are used to a process whereby both buyers and sellers instruct their own solicitors to represent them and look after their interests. But *notaires* do not represent either party in the transaction.

Although they seem like solicitors, and are often grouped together in practices (called *études*) just as they are at home, they are in fact public officials, whose duty is to the State. Their function is to ensure that the transaction is carried out legally and accurately and in due form, and therefore to give it absolute validity that cannot be contested. They are also tax collectors, in that they are responsible for collecting the equivalent of stamp duty and various other taxes due on property transactions. And one of their duties is to ensure that the change of ownership is registered with the *cadastre*, the French equivalent of the Land Registry.

It is clear then that *notaires* are essentially technicians. They are not advisers, and they will not volunteer information about the various stages of the conveyancing process. This is not to say that they are unhelpful, but simply that you must not expect them to be available at the end of a phone line to explain points to you or discuss aspects of the sale contract as your friendly family solicitor would.

To complicate the picture, *notaires* are empowered to act as estate agents by negotiating the deal as well as formalising it. They often do so, especially in country districts. Indeed until recently, when estate agents have become more common outside towns, the only way to find out about property on the market in some areas was to contact the local *notaires*. If they negotiate the deal from the outset, they are entitled to charge a fee for this work, although it will probably be lower than the estate agent's commission.

As *notaires* have a duty to be neutral, not acting for either party, only one is needed to deal with a property purchase. Ninety-five per cent of such transactions are dealt with by a single *notaire*. In practice this is generally the *notaire* who dealt with the previous sale in the case of old property, since he/she will have all the necessary documentation on file concerning such matters as the exact location and description of the property, previous owners, inheritance (if any) leading to ownership, the seller's marriage contract and so on.

But this means that the *notaire* is produced by the seller. And even though they have been told that *notaires* are neutral, many British buyers can't stop themselves feeling suspicious about this. Having been brought up with a system of a solicitor acting for each side, they feel uncomfortable especially in country districts, where the *notaire* may come from the next village and is clearly a chum of the present owner. One solution is to bring in a second *notaire* to assist the first. You are perfectly entitled to do this. It will not even increase the legal fees (which, remember, the buyer pays), as the fees must then be split between the two *notaires*. You can find a *notaire* by asking around locally or by contacting the Chambre Interdépartementale des notaires.* At one time, *notaires* were only allowed to deal with property in their own area, but this restriction has now been abolished so there is nothing to stop you using a *notaire* recommended by friends elsewhere in France, or a big practice in Paris. Estate agents and property searchers in Britain can often recommend *notaires* too.

But before you take this step, remember that the second *notaire* will still not be acting for you. He too is neutral, and will not be on hand to advise you as an English solicitor would, though he will be prepared to explain any points about which you are unclear. Even if he speaks good English, you may still find it difficult to understand some of the more complex clauses of the contract. If you have no French at all, it would be foolish to sign a contract without being sure that you know what you are letting yourself in for. Never rely on translations supplied by an agent locally or in Britain: there is no exact equivalent of many legal terms and you may be seriously misled.

Bringing in your own lawyer
If you have found your house or flat through a British agent or property searcher, they will probably be prepared to vet the contract for you. But they are not lawyers, so their advice cannot be as authoritative as that of a consultant whose services you retain for a separate fee.

Undoubtedly the most reassuring method, if you are prepared to pay for it, is to consult an international lawyer, or a British legal adviser thoroughly conversant with French conveyancing procedures. A number of British solicitors' practices have set up special services to advise clients on French property transactions. Names and addresses of some of these are given at the end of this chapter. The French Chamber of Commerce* in London and the Law Society* will supply lists of suitably qualified advisers. The Franco-British Chamber of Commerce* in Paris has details of some British lawyers or law firms working in France. You can also make contact with suitable firms by attending one of the trade shows devoted to buying property overseas (see Chapter 4).

Such advice does not come cheap (see pages 46 and 47) and if you want the adviser to be on hand when you sign the preliminary and final contracts of sale, or to sign for you via a power of attorney, you will also have to pay travel and possibly accommodation expenses. But you may well think it worth it for the peace of mind it will give you. In particular, if you are thinking of moving to France permanently at some point in the future, perhaps when you retire, it will be helpful to have someone to turn to for advice on the many complex issues involved. And lawyers of this kind will generally be able to put you in touch with tax and financial advisers if this proves necessary, as well as advising you on inheritance, Wills and other related matters.

Your decision as to whether or not to pay for this type of advice must of course be your own, and the sums involved may seem disproportionate for a tiny cottage, but long-uninhabited rural places do often cause legal problems.

It may be that, having decided not to pay for an extra legal adviser, you are faced after completion with a problem you find hard to understand. For instance, some of the land attached to your house may still be officially classified as for agricultural use, and you therefore receive a demand for higher taxes than you were expecting. Rutherfords* offer a 'troubleshooting service' to deal with just such problems, which can often be resolved rapidly with a small amount of paperwork and a few phone calls. Available to anyone who has bought a house or flat in France, it is charged on an hourly rate.

Check and double-check!

Although professional advisers clearly perform a useful (sometimes essential) service, there is no substitute for asking questions yourself, to double-check on exact procedures. I discovered this for myself when I sold my house in France before leaving the country. I had consulted a British expert living in France on a specific tax question and he had thrown in – helpfully as I thought – a warning at the end of his letter that in France you never get the proceeds of a property sale on the day the final deed is signed, but must wait at least a month. I have also seen this stated in a number of books on the subject.

Imagine, then, my surprise when, just as I was about to leave the *notaire*'s office to have a celebratory drink with the buyers after we had signed the *acte authentique*, I was called back by the kindly clerk: 'But, *Madame*, we still have a little business to transact, you and I'. I shook hands with my buyers and went back into the elegant office. Whereupon I was handed a cheque for the proceeds of the sale.

I was completely taken aback. I hadn't even decided where I was going to put the money – in a British or French bank or a British building society. Moreover, it was a Friday evening, I was due to go away for the weekend and the banks were shut on Monday. The clerk was surprised at my surprise: but of course you got the money on the day of the sale. I cursed myself for not having checked this point with him and spent the weekend worrying about what to do with the money!

Now I am aware that this does not often happen. But it did in my case. And the incident only serves to illustrate my point that you should always check exactly what will happen at each stage.

Legal costs

Legal costs, always paid by the buyer, are made up of the *notaire*'s fee for conveyancing, plus his expenses if relevant, plus various duties and taxes he has to collect.

Notaires' fees are controlled and are worked out on a complicated sliding scale consisting of a series of *tranches* or bands. The way it works out is that you pay quite a high percentage of the selling price on the first 20,000 or so francs, dropping down to less than 1 per cent for the amount over about 100,000 francs. VAT must be paid on top of the resulting figure.

But that is only the beginning. The *frais de notaire* (*notaire*'s costs) include a number of taxes and duties: a registration tax on property over five years old (VAT is already included in the selling price of property less than five years old), stamp duty (based partly on the number of pages in the final deed of sale and the number of copies required) and additional local taxes if the property has a substantial amount of land.

Then if you take out a mortgage, the *notaire* will charge another fee. This is calculated on a band principle and the percentages are lower for each band. VAT is again payable on the total. And a recording tax must also be paid, based on the total amount borrowed. If you are taking out a second mortgage you will have to pay a higher percentage in fees.

The *notaire* may also charge for some out-of-pocket expenses, especially if the property you buy is a recent inheritance, and he has to correspond with a number of heirs.

Altogether, these legal costs usually amount to somewhere between 11 and 15 per cent of the asking price on a property over five years old, about 3–4 per cent if it is less than five years old, plus fees and taxes for registering a mortgage.

Then if the *notaire* has also acted as a middleman, bringing you and the seller together, he is entitled to a further fee, corresponding to the estate agent's commission but generally lower. Typically, it will be 5 per cent on very cheap properties (up to about 175,000 francs), 2.5 per cent above that, with VAT added.

If you bring in a second *notaire*, there will be nothing extra to pay: the two split the fees.

But you will have to pay a consultancy fee on top if you use your own legal adviser. Rutherford's associate Philip Winter-Taylor* was charging a fixed fee of £350 + VAT in the spring of 1993, for advising on the conveyance of a residential property. Prettys' French Department spoke of fees ranging from about £100 + VAT for merely producing a report stating what each clause of a contract means to £500 + VAT for following the whole conveyancing through to completion on a property costing under 750,000 francs, provided the situation is straightforward; if the situation is complex, or unexpected problems are revealed, you will be advised of this before work goes ahead on sorting them out. If you decide to set up a company as a vehicle for buying a French house, or are setting up some joint-ownership structure (see Chapter 1), the fees will be higher. Some solicitors charge an hourly rate, but may be willing to work to a budget if you request this.

The conveyancing process

The legal process of buying a property in France takes place in two stages. The first stage consists of the signing of a **preliminary agreement** between buyer and seller. The second, which usually follows two to three months later, is the signing of the final contract or **deed of sale**.

But within that basic standard framework, there are a large number of differences of detail in methods of conveyancing, some of them the result of local custom or tradition. For instance, as we have seen, there is no set pattern about who pays the estate agent's commission: in some parts of the country it is the seller, in others the buyer, occasionally it is divided between the two.

You probably know General de Gaulle's famous remark about the difficulty of governing a country that has over 300 varieties of cheese. It often seems as if it has just as many ways of dealing with property buying and selling. 'I sometimes feel,' property searcher Evelyne Berthelin Ward once said to me, only half-jokingly, 'that there are as many variations on the basic theme as there are *notaires*'.

I have pointed out a number of the most common of these variants in this chapter, but rather than add a caveat after each basic procedure, I would ask you to accept that there may be some local differences and view this fact with equanimity as the other side of the coin of the big plus point of French conveyancing. For the good news is that in spite of its complexities, buying and selling property in France is much less of a nail-biting exercise than in England and Wales, since gazumping and the horrors of the broken chain cannot occur. Remember this important point as you work your way through the various procedures.

The preliminary contract

Once you have made the decision to buy a property and have agreed the price, both you and the vendor will be required to sign a document formalising this agreement and you will hand over a deposit. This is an important matter and one that should not be entered into lightly. Unlike the stage in England and Wales where you make an offer and it is accepted, this stage is binding, subject only to certain conditions. You cannot simply change your mind, pull out of the deal and have your deposit back as you can at home. If you do change your mind, you cannot necessarily be forced to go through with the sale, but you will certainly lose your deposit, and may have to pay the vendor an extra sum in compensation.

Types of preliminary contracts

The preliminary agreement can take various forms and can bear various different names, depending partly on local usage. It can be drawn up by an estate agent, or it can be a *notaire* who prepares the document and witnesses the two signatures. It can also consist of a mere exchange of letters between buyer and seller, but this method is best avoided (see below). Buying a flat or house before it is completed requires a different form of agreement, which I have dealt with separately (see below).

Once you have told an agent that you have decided to proceed with a purchase, you will probably be encouraged to sign an agreement on the spot. A document will be produced, almost certainly a printed form. The agent may refer to it simply as a *précontrat* (preliminary contract). Although this is perfectly legal, you would be well advised not to sign anything at all straight away. And an agreement drawn up by a *notaire* is anyway preferable to one prepared and witnessed solely by an agent, which is technically referred to as being *sous seing privé* (and may be referred to as *un sous-seing privé* in some parts of France).

Why should you not sign it straight away? Because, as we have seen, this agreement is binding, and you must be absolutely sure that you are aware of what you are letting yourself in for.

Why is it better to sign a preliminary agreement drawn up by a *notaire*? Because the estate agent may not have seen any evidence that the seller really is the owner of the property, or that there are no other joint owners, and may not have described it accurately or fully, especially if a piece of land is involved as well as the house or flat. This is not to say that the agent is likely to be dishonest, but that it is the *notaire*'s job to check such matters and that he/she is better qualified and equipped to do so.

If the agent produces a document to sign, you should therefore start by saying that you wish to study it very carefully before doing so, consulting a legal adviser if necessary.

The compromis de vente

This is the most common form of preliminary contract, usually abbreviated in discussions to *un compromis*. It is a mutual agreement which is binding on both parties: by signing it sellers commit themselves to selling the property to buyers at the price stated, and buyers commit themselves to buying it at that same price. Buyers must pay a deposit, usually of 10 per cent, occasionally (and particularly in the case of new property) of only 5 per cent of the agreed selling price. If buyers change their mind, they lose their deposit and will generally have to pay an additional sum in compensation to sellers. They may even be forced to go through with the sale.

The promesse de vente

This second type of preliminary contract is not binding on both parties to the same extent as the *compromis*. By signing it, vendors still commit themselves to selling the property to buyers, but this commitment takes the form of promising not to sell it to anyone else within a stated period, usually three months. Buyers do not commit themselves absolutely to buying the property. But again they must pay a deposit of 10 per cent, or occasionally 5 per cent, of the selling price, which they will forfeit if they do not go ahead with the deal within the three months.

Other types of preliminary contract

You may be asked to sign one of a number of alternative preliminary contracts. None of these is to be recommended, but you must be aware of their existence in order to avoid them.

The **offre de vente** is merely an offer to sell the property to you. It is not binding on the seller, who can withdraw without warning, perhaps after you have incurred expense in having it vetted.

The **offre d'achat** is also risky: the vendor is not committed to selling to you, but once he/she has agreed to the price you have offered, you are committed to buying.

The **échange de lettres**, as the name suggests, takes the form of a letter from each party to the other. It can lead to considerable complications.

Best advice is that you should not proceed with any of these three alternative types of preliminary agreement.

Checking the agreement

Before signing the preliminary agreement, it is essential that you should be absolutely sure what it involves. If you have decided to pay a legal adviser, you should show it to him/her straight away. Faxing will be the best solution if you are staying in France. Otherwise take it back with you to Britain to go through it with your adviser.

The same applies if you are not using a full-scale legal consultant, but the British agent or other intermediary through whom you found the property has offered to vet it for you.

Otherwise you must sit down with the document yourself and check it through very carefully indeed.

The let-out clauses

The first thing to check is the potential reasons for which the contract can be declared null and void. These are known in French as *conditions suspensives*, technically translated as 'conditions precedent', but easier to understand if called 'let-out clauses'.

Any preliminary agreement should be dependent on a number of conditions being fulfilled. If they are not fulfilled, the agreement becomes null and void, the buyer's deposit is returned and there is no compensation to pay to the seller.

The loan clause

In a standard contract, one of these let-out clauses states that the sale is conditional on the buyer being able to obtain a loan or mortgage. In other words, if you cannot obtain the loan or mortgage you are seeking, the contract is cancelled and you get your deposit back. That is why I stressed in Chapter 1 that you must decide in advance whether or not you are going to apply for funding to finance the purchase. If you say that you are not seeking a loan, this clause will be struck out. If you say that you are, you will have to state how big a loan you intend to apply for, and what the maximum monthly repayments can be. You will also have to give details of your income.

Once the vendor has seen these details, he/she may refuse to sign if he/she feels that you are seeking a loan too high for your income. On the other hand, if you try to get out of the deal on the grounds that you have been unable to obtain a loan, the vendor (or the agent or *notaire* on his/her behalf) is entitled to seek a loan for you – and you may not refuse it if it corresponds to the figures you had inserted in the preliminary contract.

The planning clause

Another standard let-out clause concerns the obtaining of a satisfactory *certificat d'urbanisme* or planning certificate. This is the result of the *notaire*'s work along the lines of the searches instigated by your solicitor in Britain before exchange of contracts. It is issued by the local planning and development office and details any planning permits concerning the building itself and its land, and any planned road building schemes or other public works affecting the actual property (but not in the vicinity, see below). If the *notaire*'s inquiries turn up something untoward, for instance that the property is affected by a road-widening scheme and is therefore subject to a compulsory purchase order, or that it is for some reason deemed unsuitable for residential purposes, you can get out of the purchase and recover your deposit.

The easements clause

Easements (*servitude* in French) is a technical term covering third-party rights over a property or some part of it. It may for instance cover a right of way, or the right of a neighbour or neighbours to use a well on your land or in your garden if the mains supply fails or a drought is officially declared. This let-out clause may be included in the planning clause. Some easements may be hundreds of years old and no longer in use, but it might be that the *notaire*'s searches will throw up something that is deemed to make the property unusable as a dwelling place, or to reduce its value substantially. If so, again you would not have to go through with the purchase.

The pre-emptive rights clause

The Société d'amenagement foncier et d'établissement rural or SAFER, a body similar to the Land Commission, has automatic pre-emptive rights over any property with land of over 2,500 square metres: for instance if it believes that it should be used only for agricultural purposes. It rarely exercises this right, but again the *notaire* must inform the SAFER, to give it a chance to object to the sale to you. If it does so, once again the agreement becomes null and void and you can recover your deposit.

Other let-out clauses

Further *conditions suspensives* can be inserted in preliminary contracts if the seller agrees. For instance, you might want to make the contract conditional on your obtaining planning permission to extend the building in some way, or to convert it into flats. Another potential let-out clause – though this would be unusual – would be to make the deal subject to a satisfactory structural survey.

The missing surveyor

You have no doubt already noticed that I have so far failed to mention a stage in property buying considered to be standard in Britain: getting the place surveyed.

Now surveys are not standard in France, and the profession of chartered surveyor as we know it does not exist. Strange as it may seem, the French buy property without having it surveyed. Indeed, they are prepared to sign an agreement that says they agree to take the property in the state it is in at the time, including any hidden defects. If they subsequently discover a major structural problem, they will occasionally try to sue the vendor and/or estate agent and bring in an *expert auprès des tribunaux*, a type of surveyor working for the courts to determine the validity of such claims. But on the whole the French, though notoriously suspicious in most of their business dealings, take things on trust when they buy a house or flat.

You cannot rely, either, on a survey being carried out by any bank to whom you apply for a loan or mortgage. French banks are traditionally more interested in your ability to make the monthly repayments than in the state of the property, taking the pragmatic view that it is worth whatever someone is prepared to pay for it. However things have changed recently, and French banks offering mortgages to British buyers will probably insist on something like the valuation survey required by British banks and building societies, or at any rate evidence of the state the place is in. However they will not require a full structural survey.

The nearest equivalent to surveyors in France are *géomètres experts*, whose main role is to check on land measurements. They are not normally called on to survey property. French buyers would be more likely to approach an architect or a specialist tradesman or craftsman if they wanted an opinion on the work that needed doing on a house or flat – a roofer, say, or a mason. But they would not ask such people to produce a detailed report such as a British surveyor prepares.

Finding a surveyor

If you feel uncomfortable about adopting a 'when in Rome' policy and prefer to follow the British practice of having the property surveyed, you will need to give some thought to finding a surveyor.

One method is to turn to a surveyor you have already used at home. Remember that you will have to pay his travelling and other expenses as well as the survey fee. And although it will be reassuring to have the opinion of someone you know, he is unlikely to be familiar with French building techniques and materials. Moreover, he will not be able to give you an idea of the cost of any work he believes needs doing: he will not know about local building regulations and official standards, about labour costs, or about availability and cost of materials.

Another solution is to look in the specialist property magazines (see Chapter 4). Here you sometimes find advertisements from British surveyors, some of them living in France. It would be wise to ask for a reference from a British client who has had a similar survey prepared. If the surveyor is based in Britain, or in another part of France, you will again have travelling and other expenses to pay.

If you have found the property through British agents, they may be able to recommend a surveyor. And as French agents are now aware of the anxieties experienced by their British clients on the survey question, many have compiled lists of local *géomètres experts* and builders willing to do a full structural survey – usually rather expensively. But in both cases you must reassure yourself about their independence. Ask yourself whether you would feel happy about having a British property surveyed by a surveyor recommended by the agent who is hoping to sell it to you.

Another potential source is a legal consultant who is advising you on the purchase. Such consultants specialising in French conveyancing can often put you in touch with a surveyor, just as your solicitor would at home.

You could also ask around in the area for a recommendation to a local French *géomètre expert*, architect or builder, or get a list of local members from the Ordre des géomètres experts* in Paris. But even if you speak good French, you will no doubt find it difficult to follow the survey report in detail. To have it translated would only add to the expense, and you would have to be very sure that the translator was competent in this specialised field. Moreover the French surveyor or builder may not have the same standards as you in relation to, say, wiring and plumbing (see Chapter 5).

Yet another solution is to try to find, perhaps through the local British community, a recommended British surveyor, architect, builder or other suitable person living in the area, and used to dealing with local workmen and craftsmen. This is usually the best answer to the problem: no, or minimal, travelling expenses, a report that you will understand, a respect for British standards of comfort and convenience, knowledge of local techniques, materials and prices – and of good local builders. For such a person will also be very handy if and when you need help with finding local builders and supervising their work.

A useful service of this kind is supplied by David Marr Limited* in the southwest, who, after supervising the restoration of many buildings in Britain and Canada, are now based in the Tarn-et-Garonne *département* and operating throughout the south-west. They carry out surveys for British would-be buyers, supply detailed costings for work that will need doing and, if requested, commission and supervise work from their tried-and-tested team of craftsmen (see Chapter 5). They charge either on an hourly basis, roughly equivalent in 1993 to £15 per hour or, on a large project, a percentage of the building costs; and they, or someone like them in other regions, should ensure that you are fully aware of what you will be letting yourself in for when you contemplate buying a property.

Deciding on a survey

When you need to decide whether or not to have the house or flat surveyed, and if so at what stage, an experience of my own may be helpful. We once saw a large house in France that was exactly what we had been looking for for over a year. I felt the usual British urge to have it surveyed before we committed ourselves. But it was August and the surveyor I had used in Britain was on holiday. My husband, being French, was quite used to the idea of buying without a survey. We had heard about the house, which was very attractive, just before it officially came on the market and knew that if we hesitated we might lose it. So we went ahead, expecting merely to have to do some minor modernisation to bathroom and kitchen as well as redecorating and turning two small rooms into one big one.

But when we got in a plumber to quote for redoing the bathroom and an electrician to put in some extra power points, we got some unpleasant surprises. Eventually we had to have the whole place replumbed and rewired, which meant ripping out wooden casings and causing a great deal of damage, necessitating replastering and the like. It all cost very much more and took up far more time than we had anticipated.

Now I never regretted buying that house. It was exactly what we wanted and we were very happy there. But I did very much regret not having found out in advance what was involved, and been able to plan accordingly. I had to give up working for a bit to supervise the various workmen and it complicated our lives considerably.

So my advice must be that you should at least find out what costs, if any, are likely to be involved. A full structural survey must be the ideal. But if you have really fallen in love with the place and feel certain that you will lose it if you delay – objectively certain, not just because the agent is pressurising you – then look at the property very carefully and calmly, reading Chapter 5 first to see what type of work may be needed and to get some idea of cost. If you are still sure it is your dream home, try to get a 'subject to survey' let-out clause added to the preliminary contract. If that works, well and good, sign the contract and go ahead and commission the survey. If it fails, take a deep breath and sign anyway, but do still get some-one in to give you an estimate for the extent and cost of any work needed.

Checking through the preliminary agreement

The exact wording of the preliminary agreement will vary, and the whole document will be longer and more detailed if it is drawn up by a *notaire*, rather than a printed form produced by an agent. But it should contain, as well as the let-out clauses I have already referred to, the following details, not necessarily in this order:

1) Full details of both buyer and seller, including dates of birth, occu-pation, address, the type of marriage contract if relevant, nationality, non-residence in France if applicable.

2) A detailed description of the property, including the number of rooms on each floor and their use, and the Land Registry number for each parcel of land. If the property, or part of it (for instance a separate garage) is in a jointly owned building or complex of buildings, details of the co-owners' regulations will follow, plus information such as whether or not water is supplied to a garage.

3) In a *notaire*'s contract there will be full details of previous sales or inheritances leading to the property being owned by the current seller.

4) The date when the preliminary agreement is to be completed by the signing of the final deed of sale. This date is generally eight to twelve weeks away. There will normally be a sentence stipulating that the date can be brought forward if the buyers wish, but that they must give the sellers two weeks' notice of this in writing, by registered letter.

5) The buyers' obligations. These may state that even if the completion date is brought forward, the sellers must be allowed to continue to use the premises until the initially agreed date; that the buyers agree to take the building in the state in which they find it on completion; that they accept any easements; that they will make sure that the sellers are not pestered by the local authorities or an insurance company over contracts for electricity, gas, water or insurance (buyers are supposed to deal with such matters before completion) and pay any sums due for such services and any local taxes from the day they take possession; and that they will pay all legal costs involved in the transaction.

As I have pointed out, let-out clauses may affect the agreements to take the property in the state in which it is found and the matter of ease-ments.

6) Among various statements by the sellers concerning their title to the property and their obligations, it should be stated that the property comes with vacant possession and is free of encumbrances. Check also that details are given of who is to pay for any work due to be carried out under a *copropriété* agreement. It may be stipulated that any such work previously agreed is to be paid for by the sellers, even if it has not been started at the date of completion. This is obviously preferable to a situation where the sellers are liable only for work already under way on

completion. Check this carefully, and double-check with the *syndic* (see Chapter 1) that you have been made aware of all decisions concerning work not yet started.

7) The sum to be paid as a deposit and to whom it is payable. It is preferable to pay this to a *notaire*. The origin of the funds, if they come from a non-resident source, has traditionally been included, to ensure that they can be taken out of France if and when the property is sold. Exchange controls were abolished some years ago, but many *notaires* will still include it, and it certainly cannot do any harm to have it in.

8) The let-out clauses already referred to.

9) A statement, if relevant, that the buyers are not intending to seek a loan, and that they recognise that if they change their mind on this point, a let-out clause concerning a loan cannot be inserted later. The wording of this statement will be inserted in their own handwriting at the end of the agreement by buyers not seeking a loan.

10) Alternatively, details of the loan being sought, the buyers' income, the monthly repayments and the various dates by which the buyers must either obtain a loan or inform the sellers that they have been unable to do so.

11) The name and address of the *notaire* who will be drawing up the final sale deed, and, if relevant, of the second *notaire*.

12) If the sale has been negotiated by an intermediary (estate agent or *notaire*) the commission due to that intermediary and whether it is payable by the buyer, the seller, or shared between them.

This may be followed by a statement that if both parties come to an amicable agreement not to go through with the sale, the intermediary will receive a specific sum in compensation. A rider may be added to the effect that if the sale is reactivated within a certain period, the commission will be due in full. This reflects agents' understandable irritation when attempts are made to evade the commission by a pretence that the sale is off, followed, after a decent interval, by a private agreement between the same two parties.

13) A final clause may appear stating that both parties declare that the contract represents the full price agreed between them. This is, of course, to discourage 'under the table' agreements (see below).

Check the date of the contract carefully. If the seller has already signed it, the contract date should not be that date, but the later date when you sign it.

Other points to check before signing
Plots
It is very important to check that the right parcels of land are referred to in the contract. If necessary, go back to have another look at the property, especially where various fields or bits of land are involved. If you have to bring in a land surveyor to confirm the exact boundaries, you will have to pay his or her fee, which is likely to be in the region of 4000 francs.

Roads

Presumably the last thing you want is a motorway shattering the peace of your new-found French retreat. But finding out about the likelihood of such a catastrophe may not be so easy. Although it is often said that the *notaire* does the equivalent of a solicitor's local searches, his are much more limited: he obtains information only about the property you are buying, and will not draw your attention to the fact that a motorway spur is to be built a couple of hundred yards away.

The French are not as a rule good about getting together to set up campaign committees to protest about proposed new developments. So don't count on being made aware of a new road scheme as you would be in Britain, where vociferous posters and banners will sprout along roadsides and in villages. Moreover, the local people, frustrated for years at having to drive long distances along slow roads, may welcome a motorway or major trunk road. And in poor rural areas where there are few job opportunities for young people, there may well be understandable enthusiasm at the prospects opened up by a new road scheme (work in petrol stations or roadside restaurants). As Frank Rutherford points out, local authorities even produce glossy brochures boasting of driving a five-lane highway through everyone's back yard!

To solve the problem of finding out about such developments, Rutherfords* offer a useful service called a Road Search. The service carries full legal protection and is covered by indemnity insurance. For a fee of £55 (1993 prices) you will be sent a map (scale 1:50,000) of the area round your prospective house or flat showing the route of any proposed new major roads.

As for other new developments like golf courses or leisure centres, you could always try asking at the local *mairie*; and looking in the local paper and talking to future neighbours might elicit some information.

Listed buildings and areas

It is common in France for whole districts, as well as individual buildings, to be listed (*classés*). This may apply, for instance, to the centre of a historic town. This will mean that any work you want to do on it will be particularly strictly controlled: obtaining planning permission may be difficult, and will certainly be long drawn out. If the building itself, or part of it, is a *monument historique*, you will be subject to all sorts of rules and regulations and compulsory inspections. Check with the local *mairie* and, if necessary with the Caisse nationale des Monuments historiques.*

Don't go under the table!

Do not, repeat not, let the seller persuade you into handing over some of the agreed sum in cash 'under the table', on the pretext that the legal costs and the commission will therefore be lower.

For a start, this is illegal. If you are still tempted – or if the seller tries to force you into it by threatening to withdraw from the sale of a property you have set your heart on – consider the dangers. Firstly, when you come to sell your house or flat, your capital gains tax liability will be increased if the purchase price given in the sale deeds was too low (see Chapter 8). Secondly, you may finish up losing both the house or flat and some of your money. This is because if the local tax office suspect some fiddle has been going on, they are entitled, during the six months after completion, to issue the equivalent of a compulsory purchase order at a price 10 per cent above the figure given in the sale deed. The chances of your ever getting your money back from the seller in such circumstances must be reckoned to be slim.

Needless to say, if you ever tried to buy property again in France, the tax authorities would view you with suspicion.

Signing the preliminary contract

Once you have examined the preliminary contract very carefully indeed, taken legal advice, made all the extra checks I have referred to, including a survey if you have decided to commission one, and visited the house or flat again to make absolutely sure that it is right for you, you are ready to take the plunge and sign the contract. If you are still in France at this point, you can simply go to the agent's or *notaire*'s office and sign it. If you have returned home you can post or fax it. But the document does not become binding until the deposit has reached the *notaire*'s account, or that of the agent acting as stakeholder.

Paying the deposit

The simplest way of paying the deposit is to have a French bank account and to give or send a cheque in French francs.

If you have not yet opened a bank account, or your first cheque book has still failed to materialise, you can arrange for an inter-bank telex transfer to be sent from your British bank to the account of the *notaire* or agent who will be receiving it. Your bank will probably tell you that this takes only forty-eight hours. Experience suggests that you should allow at least six working days; best allow ten days to make sure that it has transited via Paris to the regional branch and then to the *notaire*'s account. Telex transfers do occasionally disappear into the banking system for a while, but they can never be lost entirely. On the other hand the third alternative, a banker's draft drawn in French francs on your British account, can cause problems unless you hand it over in person: it may get lost in the post, and there is no procedure for you to put a stop on it as you can with a cheque. You will have to get the money to France by some other method, but your account will already have been debited and you will have to wait some time for reimbursement. And meanwhile, you may have lost your proposed purchase because the seller has lost patience.

Some *notaires* and agents will accept travellers' cheques in francs or Eurocheques.

After the preliminary contract

During the period between the signing of the preliminary contract and completion of the transaction you will probably hear nothing from the *notaire*. But he/she will be dealing with matters such as checking the vendor's title to the property, obtaining a planning certificate, having a plan drawn up if a parcel of land is to be divided, informing the SAFER about the proposed sale, making sure that any mortgage on the property will be cleared, and then drawing up the *acte de vente* or *acte authentique*, the final conveyance document.

It is essential that you and your adviser should see a draft of this sale deed before completion and check it through carefully to make sure that it is complete and accurate. Make this clear from the outset so that you do not have to check everything in a rush at the time of completion. Nowadays most *notaires* will be able to fax it to you or to your adviser. You should also be sent a *plan cadastral* (a sketch extracted from the Land Registry) so that you can check that the right parcels of land are included in country properties.

Meanwhile there are various things that you must get on with yourself. The most urgent is the mortgage, if you intend to obtain one. You must set this in motion straight away, as if you fail to obtain one, you must inform the seller and the agent and *notaire* of this within a set period in order to benefit from the let-out clause. Assuming that you do get the mortgage, you will need to send the details to the *notaire*, or to an agent acting as your adviser or a legal adviser, so that they can be included in the conveyance document. You will also need to take out life insurance from the moment you accept the offer of a mortgage. The lender should send you the necessary forms for this.

Insurance

The lender may also include in its information pack a proposal form for household insurance, from a French insurance group. This is the next item you must deal with, to ensure that the property is covered on completion. You will have to send the *notaire* details of the policy you take out, as it is one of his duties to check that the place is insured. Under French law you must be insured against third-party damage as well as fire and other risks.

Insurance on holiday homes is not always easy to arrange for those resident outside France. French insurance companies traditionally offer their regular clients special low rates on second homes because they are handling all their insurance on their main home, their cars, their dogs and so on. It is clearly not in their interest to offer you these low rates when they are not part of a package. Moreover holiday homes owned by non-residents are liable to be left unoccupied for longer periods than those visited most weekends by French families, and are therefore more of an insurance risk.

If you are not borrowing from a French bank, or they cannot help you, a

British agent or middleman through whom you buy may be able to give you the names and addresses of insurance companies willing to insure that type of property. So may a French agent, particularly in a region where there are many non-resident owners and the local insurers have latched on to this market. In fact some estate agents are also insurance agents. Another alternative is to ask your British insurance company to effect the cover for you, probably via Lloyd's.

You will have to fill in a complex proposal form that will ask all sorts of questions about how often the house or flat will be left unoccupied. It will also ask for details of locks and other forms of protection. French insurance policies generally include detailed provisions about protection. You are normally expected to have at least two locks on all doors, one of a mortice type, although window locks are rare because shutters make them redundant. The policy may state that for cover above a certain sum, as many as three locks are required on all doors. In high-risk areas, especially in towns, you may be required to install a specially reinforced door called a *porte blindée*.

It will probably also specify that all forms of protection on doors are to be used at all times when the place is empty, and that all other forms of protection must be used after 10 p.m., and during the day as well if the premises are unoccupied for more than two days. Like many Britons, you may suspect that the practice of leaving shutters firmly closed when you are away, thus advertising your absence to all and sundry, is one reason behind the high rate of burglaries in France. But if you leave the shutters hinged back or rolled up and the place is burgled, the insurance company probably won't pay up.

As ever in bureaucratic France, insurance companies are liable to have complicated premium scales. You may, for instance, be asked whether your new French home is of type A, B or C. Classification will depend on criteria such as whether or not a block of flats has a marble entrance hall. Premiums are likely to be higher than you are used to.

Completion

Signing of the *acte de vente* takes place in the *notaire*'s office. You may well want to be in on this rather impressive moment, as the *notaire* solemnly reads out what is often a very lengthy document and buyers and sellers solemnly listen. It has a somewhat Dickensian feel to it, and I have always felt that it would be more appropriate if I was handing over a bag of gold rather than a mundane cheque or banker's draft. It certainly provides you with an interesting insight into French mentalities and ways of conducting transactions affecting their *patrimoine* or heritage, a sacred concept in France. And you may find yourselves, especially in country areas, setting the seal on the beginning of your new French adventure with a gargantuan celebratory meal with the vendors.

If you have no time to travel to France to enjoy this little bit of ceremony you can arrange for a power of attorney to be granted to a legal adviser, or simply to a clerk in the *notaire*'s office. You must sign the power of attorney at a French consulate in Britain or at a *notaire*'s office in France.

The *notaire* will need to see various documents at the time of the signature: birth certificates, marriage certificates if relevant, divorce papers if relevant, and passports for all purchasers. You must either take along (or give to your attorney) a banker's draft for the completion price, or arrange for a telex transfer, or draw a cheque on your French bank account if you have been able to transfer enough funds in advance. The price will be the remaining 90 or 95 per cent of the agreed sale price, the fees and taxes payable on the sale and the additional fees and registration taxes on the mortgage if you have one. The *notaire* will have sent you or your legal adviser a statement setting out these various figures, so that you can ensure that the necessary funds due from you and from the bank providing you with a mortgage are received in time.

Some of the figures are only estimates, as the exact amounts of tax and duties payable will not be known until all the registration has been completed. With a bit of luck, you will get a small refund from the *notaire* in due course.

After completion
The *notaire* must now deal with various formalities like registering the sale deed with the Land Registry. Some weeks or even months later you will receive a certified copy of the title document, but you do not have a bundle of title deeds of the type that you would give to your solicitor or bank for safekeeping at home. Evidence of title is recorded in the Land Registry.

Buying on plan
If you are buying a flat or house in a new development before it has been completed (see Chapter 1) the procedure is not quite the same as with 'resale' property (i.e. property that has had a previous owner). This type of purchase is very common in France and strictly regulated by law to ensure that developers do not exploit their clients. It is also referred to by the term 'off plan'.

The preliminary contract is called a *contrat de réservation* and, as with resale purchases, is binding. But a number of conditions must be fulfilled, so you have the equivalent of various let-out clauses as well as the standard clause about obtaining a loan. For instance, if the final price is more than 5 per cent higher than the original price quoted, or the developer does not complete the sale by the due date, or one or more of the services to be supplied does not materialise, or there is a clear discrepancy between the original description and the final state of the house or flat, the contract becomes null and void and your deposit will be returned, unless of course you are happy to go ahead in these changed circumstances.

The deposit is much lower than for an older property: in fact, under recent legislation, a system of deposits up to a maximum of 3 per cent. Also new is the 'guarantee of completion' (*garantie de parfait achèvement*), which means that the builder is legally required to provide a surety bond given by a bank or insurance company to cover buyers against poor workmanship or against the work not being completed. A series of stage payments will be set out in the *contrat de réservation*, to be made as the development progresses. You must have the preliminary contract vetted carefully to make sure that the communal services described in the accompanying details will be adequate and that you understand exactly what you will be buying.

The developer will usually expect his *notaire* to be used for the conveyance. If you feel uneasy about this, you must bring in a second *notaire* and/or your own legal adviser. As with older properties, the *notaire* prepares the final conveyance document, which must be signed in the same way. The legal fees and title registration fee must be paid on completion of the purchase (which may occur well before completion of the house or flat), along with the relevant stage payment. But there is no registration tax on this type of property, as instead VAT is included in the purchase price.

Mortgages on this type of purchase are very common, with extra legal fees and taxes to be paid in the same way as with older property.

When the building is eventually finished, it is standard practice to leave 5 per cent off the last stage payment to enable you to reassure yourself that the work has been completed to your satisfaction. You would be wise to bring in a surveyor or architect at this stage to check on the technical aspects. If anything still needs doing or modifying, make sure that it is done before you hand over that last 5 per cent. The basic structural work comes with a ten-year guarantee, and you are entitled to get the developer to put right any defects of a less major nature over a two-year period. But it is still a wise precaution to insist on outstanding matters being cleared up before you have lost the lever of the 5 per cent you have held back.

A final comment

You may have been told by French friends that *notaires* are impossibly slow. British books on the subject also tend to say that French *notaires* don't seem to see conveyancing as having any degree of urgency. In fact the overall image is of someone rather stuffy and fuddy-duddy, who needs hurrying along.

My own dealings with *notaires* have always given the lie to this, and I know many British families who have found, like me, that conveyancing, and any other legal work, goes through faster and more smoothly in France than in Britain. When I remarked once to a *notaire*'s clerk that I thought his profession's reputation for slowness quite undeserved, he replied with a sad smile: 'But what you have to remember, *Madame*, is that in French families, you usually find that at least two of the members aren't speaking to each other. That always slows things up'.

Of course you may be unlucky enough to buy from just such a family – particularly if the property has recently been inherited by several joint heirs. But on the whole the conveyancing system militates in favour of a speedy conclusion. It should also be said that things will probably proceed more quickly if you have taken on a legal adviser, unless your French is really good and you can keep chivvying as necessary.

Making a French Will

Your assets in France automatically come under French inheritance laws, so it makes sense to look into these carefully while you are waiting for completion of the sale, and act accordingly. If you are paying a legal consultant to advise you on the sale purchase, he will also be able to help you here.

The main point to remember is that you cannot simply make up your own mind who you are going to leave your new French home to. In Britain you can favour one of your children or leave all your assets and worldly goods to your faithful cleaning lady or a hospice or a cats' home. They order things differently in France. Laws designed to protect the family, and, initially, in the period following the French Revolution, to break up large estates so that no one landowner could become too powerful, make it compulsory to leave a specific proportion of your estate to your children in equal shares. Thus if you have one child, half your estate must go to him or her. If you have two children, they are entitled to a third each. If you have three, they each get a quarter. That means that you are free to choose how to leave half, a third and a quarter of your estate respectively.

If one or more of your children is already dead, his/her children must inherit the prescribed share. If you have no children, the direct line principle goes upwards instead of downwards and the first claim on your estate is your parents'.

A surviving spouse does not have any such rights, but may be entitled to an outright inheritance or a life interest, depending on the marriage *régime* you are deemed to enjoy in the absence of a French-style marriage contract. Moreover, a surviving spouse is not allowed to sell a property in France without the agreement of any surviving descendants (children or grandchildren) and ascendants (parents or grandparents). This can cause serious problems if your children are minors (under 18) at the time of your death.

There are various ways of mitigating these effects but they tend to be expensive. They include buying through a company (see Chapter 1) and joint purchases (known as buying *en tontine* and generally advantageous on second homes only if the value of the property is quite low). It is essential that you get expert legal and financial advice before embarking on any such steps.

You will probably not be surprised to hear that death duties, or inheritance duties (*droits de succession*) as the French prefer to think of them, are also governed by complex regulations and scales of payment. The basic principle is that the closer the family relationship between the beneficiary and the deceased, the lower the duty payable. But there is no exemption, as there is in Britain, for spouses.

Inheritance duties are payable by anyone who inherits property in France, no matter where he/she is resident. After various allowances (most generous in the case of spouses, children and parents, non-existent for those who are not relations) the duty operates on a series of bands, starting at 5 per cent for spouses, children and parents, rising to 40 per cent on large assets; at 35 per cent for brothers and sisters, rising to 45 per cent. Before deciding to leave your French home to a friend because you have no children, pause to consider that your friendly gesture may turn out to be what the French call a *cadeau empoisonné*, a poisoned gift: inheritance duty of 60 per cent will be payable on its value.

In view of the differences between the two methods of dealing with inheritance in France and Britain, and the expense involved in applying an English Will in France, it will make things simpler for your heirs if you make a separate Will in France covering your French home. To make things simpler for yourself, you need merely write out (do not type) the details and sign and date it. This is known as a holograph Will (*testament olographe*) and it must not be witnessed. You can ask a *notaire* or legal adviser for suitable wording if you wish and it is wise to leave it with a *notaire*, and give the details to your solicitor in Britain. Keep a photocopy for yourself and let your family know what you have done.

A holograph Will is perfectly adequate, but if you prefer you can make a formal *testament authentique*: two *notaires* must witness it (or one *notaire* and at least two other witnesses). If you are determined to keep the contents secret, you can make a *testament mystique* or *testament secret*: you write it and then sign it, put it into an envelope and seal it in the presence of two witnesses, then hand it over to a *notaire*.

You can get advice from a British lawyer, or an experienced estate agent, such as Rutherfords*, who offer a Will Service, which cost £95 in 1993 (or £175 for two people). Your intentions will be drafted into French for you and you then copy out the wording. You will also be given a checklist for your executors, so that they will know how to proceed. Do also consult your own solicitor about the advisability of revising your English Will to exclude any French assets.

Moving furniture to France

Once you are at last the proud owner of your new French home you will probably be eager to get it furnished. Even if you must first launch into extensive restoration, it will be fun to think about getting it ready to live in. But don't rush into it. Thanks to the Single European Market, you no longer need to worry about customs controls, but moving furniture abroad is still an expensive business.

There is a lot to be said for starting off by buying garden furniture locally and using that indoors until you have decided what to bring over or what to buy specially for the new place. (But see Chapter 6 for a warning about looking for suitable local pieces.) You can take over kettles and other small equipment (but again see Chapter 6 for a warning about using

French electricity) and buy kitchen and bathroom basics in a local supermarket or hardware store. Then decide when you are spending your first holiday there what type of furniture and furnishings will be suitable for the climate and for the lifestyle you intend to lead. You will, for instance, be spending a great deal of time out of doors if you are mainly using the place for summer holidays. If you intend to use it for frequent short breaks, your furniture and other needs will be different. Thanks to the virtually universal presence of shutters, you do not need to rush into deciding on curtain fabrics either. Kitchen appliances and bathroom equipment are best bought locally (see Chapter 5).

If you decide to take furniture over from Britain, you can probably transport small items a few at a time when you are driving over for a holiday. But for large items you must use an international removal firm or hire a van yourself, provided you have some strong helpers. Van-hire firms do not usually allow you to hire in one country and leave the vehicle in another, so you will either have to hire a van from somewhere near your French home and drive it to Britain empty, then return with it loaded up, or hire in Britain and return it empty. Don't forget to take out adequate insurance.

International removal firms are generally expensive, but if you pick a thoroughly experienced firm (the French consulate may be able to advise you, or check out firms exhibiting at French property exhibitions or advertising in specialist magazines), you will have a lot of effort and worry taken off your shoulders. The abolition of customs controls for EC citizens means that you no longer need to spend time drawing up inventories. However, as silver clouds usually do have dark linings, now that Europe is a Single Market, you will have to pay VAT on the removal firm's bill.

Finding a legal adviser

The Law Society
113 Chancery Lane
London WC2
tel: 071-242 1222

Chambre Interdépartmentale des Notaires
12 av. Victoria
75001 Paris
Write here with an international reply coupon for the address of the (Chambre départmentale des notaires), which can supply names and addresses of local *notaires*.

Chambre de Commerce française de Grande-Bretagne
Knightsbridge House
197 Knightsbridge
London SW7 1RB
tel: 071-225 5235
fax: 071-225 5557

Franco-British Chamber of Commerce
8 rue Cimarosa
75016 Paris
tel: (010-33-1) 44-05-32-88
fax: (010-33-1) 44-05-32-99

Some British law firms

A non-exhaustive list of lawyers in Britain able to offer a full consultancy service on French property buying and related matters such as inheritance:

Sean O'Connor
4 River Walk
Tonbridge
Kent TN9 1DT
tel: Tonbridge (0732) 365 378
fax: Tonbridge (0732) 360 144

Osborne Clarke
30 Queen Charlotte Street
Bristol BS99 7QQ
tel: Bristol (0272) 230 220
fax: Bristol (0272) 279 209

and

6–9 Middle Street
London EC1A 7JA
tel: 071-600 0155
fax: 071-726 2772

Pannone & Partners
41 Spring Gardens
Manchester M2 2BB
tel: 061-832 3000
fax: 061-834 2064

and

14 New Street
London EC2M 4TR
tel: 071-972 9720
fax: 071-972 9724

De Pinna, Scorers & John Venn
3 Albemarle Street
London W1X 3HF
tel: 071-409 3188
fax: 071-355 1596

Penningtons
Dashwood House
69 Old Broad Street
London EC2M 1PE
tel: 071-457 3000
fax: 071-457 3240

and

7 rue La Fayette
75009 Paris
France
tel: (010-33-1) 48-78-00-24
fax: (010-33-1) 40-23-95-46

Prettys Solicitors
Elm House
25 Elm Street
Ipswich
Suffolk IP1 2AD
tel: Ipswich (0473) 232 121
fax: Ipswich (0473) 230 002

Russell-Cooke Potter & Chapman
French Department
2 Putney Hill
London SW15 6AB
tel: 081-789 9111
fax: 081-788 1299

and

Villantipolis 5
Route des Dolines
Sophia-Antipolis
06560 Valbonne
France
tel: (010-33) 93-65-31-18
fax: (010-33) 92-96-07-23

Philip Winter-Taylor
40 Englefield Road
Theale RG7 5AS
tel: Reading (0734) 323 719
fax: Reading (0734) 323 695

Other useful addresses

French consulates
London
21 Cromwell Road
London SW7 2EN
tel: 071-581 5292

Edinburgh
11 Randolph Crescent
Edinburgh EH3 7TT
tel: 031-225-7954

Jersey
La Motte Street
St Hélier
Jersey JE2 4SY
tel: Jersey (0534) 26256

**Caisse nationale des Monuments
historiques**
Hôtel de Sully
62 rue Saint-Antoine
75004 Paris
tel: (010-33-1) 44-61-20-00

Ordre des Géomètres Experts
40 av. Hoche
75008 Paris
tel: (010-33-1) 45-63-24-26
fax: (010-33-1) 45-61-14-07

4   FINDING YOUR HOME

Once you have decided on the region that will be right for you and have a firm grasp of what buying a French house or flat involves, you have a choice of various approaches to househunting: through a French estate agent or *notaire*, through a British agent or solicitor, through various other types of intermediary in Britain or France, through advertisements in British newspapers or specialist magazines, through French newspapers or magazines, through the Minitel screen of friends in France, or of course through friends or the local British community.

Through a French estate agent direct

French estate agents operate rather differently from their British counterparts. They are on the whole less inclined to the hard sell and this, plus the need for them to have some training and/or professional qualification to obtain their licence, means that the profession does not have the somewhat dubious reputation acquired by some British agents during the property booms of the seventies and eighties.

They may seem at first less professional. They rarely compile lists of available properties for you to go through and, although things have changed a bit recently, especially in regions where the British have bought extensively, the information they give you is liable to be sketchy. Room measurements are a rarity, and descriptions are decidedly brief, of the 'charming stone house with period features and a fine view' variety. But anyone who has been bombarded with weekly lists of houses or flats, 99 per cent of which bear no resemblance to what you are looking for, knows that the saturation British method can be counter-productive. French estate agents carry a lot of information in their heads and will often be able to come up with two or three places that really do correspond to what you have asked for, even if all they can show you in the office is a dog-eared index card and a poor photograph.

An increasing number of agents in areas popular with the British now have at least one British resident working for them, probably on a commission basis, whose specific role is to deal with clients from Britain, show them over houses and flats, explain buying procedures and help them with all the formalities involved. Partly under the influence of such people, French agents are becoming better organised than a few years ago. You will probably spot a fax in one corner, and may be handed reasonably comprehensive individual information sheets in English, with a colour photograph. Measurements will still not be included, but this is mainly because the French do not think in terms of size of rooms but of overall surface area. Flats are described as being of so many square metres; with houses, this may be broken down into floors. Another difference: whereas in Britain you are used to being told the number of bedrooms, in France the total number of rooms (excluding kitchen, bathroom and lavatory) is given. In the case of flats the number may be preceded by an F or T. So 'appartement F4' means a four-roomed flat.

The better organised agencies now have fat files for clients to browse through, often with individual information sheets classified in price order. If you respond to an advertisement from a French agency in a British newspaper or magazine, you will probably receive a brief information sheet first, followed up, if you express real interest, by a colour photo or photocopy. (Colour photos and photocopies are expensive, and, because many initial inquiries lead to nothing, agents are understandably reluctant to send them in the first place.)

Agents used to dealing with British clients are becoming increasingly willing to state honestly what needs doing to a house in the country. Aware than many househunters have a shock when they see that what sounds like a charming little cottage needs virtually building from scratch inside, or discover that even quite grand houses may have no proper bathroom, they sensibly realise that rather than putting people off the whole idea of buying in France, it is better to provide a list of what will have to be attended to. Even if no list is offered, do make it clear how much work, if any, you are willing to take on, so that neither your time nor theirs is wasted.

You will have seen from the previous chapter that agent's commissions are considerably higher than you are used to at home. In return, they do much more for you than a standard British agent would. As well as helping you with the legal formalities, they will be prepared to assist you in getting a mortgage, and insurance cover. Many will book you a hotel room when you come over to househunt or to deal with the various formalities. As completion day approaches, they will check that water and electricity contracts in your name have been dealt with. They will also put you in touch with builders to estimate for renovation or restoration and, although they clearly can't act as site managers, may offer to keep an eye on any work being done while you are back in Britain. They may also be able to give you the name of rental agencies if you want to let your new home.

Finding French agents

A considerable number of French estate agents advertise in the British national press and in the specialist property magazines (see below). Once you are in France, you can look in the local paper, and get hold of the free sheets that are pushed through letterboxes all over France. Towns large and small in areas popular with second-home buyers will have several estate agents dealing mainly in this sort of property: you will soon spot them as you stroll round places like Périgueux or Cahors, Rouen or Saint-Malo. Those used to dealing with foreign clients have good clear photographs in the window so that you can get an idea of the type of property they handle. Those dealing mainly with a local clientele are liable to have old-fashioned-looking windows with a couple of dog-eared photographs. Don't forget to look for the letters FNAIM (see Chapter 3). There are several national networks of estate agents, like Agences no. 1, Avis and Century 21. Each member of the chain should be able to give you the address of other members in a different region, if you decide to look elsewhere, and they undertake a certain amount of joint advertising. But as each agency is a franchise operation, the service, even if superficially standardised, will vary depending on the management and staff: efficiency and warmth of welcome in one outlet does not guarantee that you will encounter the same in another under the same banner.

You can write to the local branch of the FNAIM* for addresses of member agencies in the area that interests you.

Opening times

Typical opening hours for estate agents are 9 or 9.30 a.m. to 12 noon and 2 or 2.30 p.m. to 6.30 or 7 p.m., Tuesday to Saturday. In large towns agents may also be open on Monday afternoon, but may close on Saturday afternoon, or even all day Saturday. As French agents virtually always accompany their clients on visits, you may find only a secretary in the office if you turn up without an appointment. It is always advisable to give several days' notice of your arrival, so that the agent can plan a series of visits for you.

The 'bon de visite'

Before visiting a property you may be asked by the agent to sign and date a chit, generally entitled a *bon de visite*. This states that the details of the property referred to in the appropriate box were given to you by the agent, whose name appears at the top, usually in the form of a stamp; that you knew of its existence solely from that source; and that if anyone else shows you the same property, you will make it clear that your first knowledge of it came from the agent. It will probably also say that you agree not to deal directly with the vendor, perhaps for a fixed period (typically three years).

Do not be alarmed by this document. The agent is merely – and understandably – protecting his commission. With the same property often on many agents' books, he wants to make sure that a colleague doesn't try to claim you first saw it through him. If he has sole agency – rare, especially in country districts – he may not bother with this document. But he is still faced with the possibility of the vendor doing a deal direct with you at some later date. The French do not on the whole care for middlemen and even otherwise honest people are liable to try to get out of paying the agent's commission.

If you are given the keys to a property to enable you to visit it by yourself, don't be surprised if the agent asks for your passport, saying he will return it when you bring the keys back. Sad to say, some British househunters have given their compatriots a bad name by walking off with keys, although agents generally admit that this seems to be through carelessness, or a failure to realise the distance needed to drive back with keys, rather than real dishonesty.

Some do's and don'ts

Do keep appointments, or cancel them if you change your mind or can't get there in time. British agents report that as many as 30 per cent of the appointments they make for their clients with French agents are not kept. An appointment made by a British agent will always be with someone who speaks at least some English, so not speaking the language is no excuse for not telephoning to cancel.

Don't do your househunting in the summer if you can possibly avoid it. Cruising around in an estate agent's car enjoying the countryside seems to have become a habit for some people during their summer holidays. So few sales result from such visits that agents are now very wary of would-be purchasers who appear at that time. You will get a much better reception in the winter, or early spring and late autumn, when the serious house-hunters move into action. Anyway, buying a place you have seen only in summer sunshine is never wise.

Do check on public holidays before planning a visit. Estate agents, like other businesses, are normally closed then. Moreover when a public holiday falls close to a weekend, or to the traditional Monday closure, a *pont* (bridge) joining the day off to standard closing days will be observed. Thus outside large towns, where Sunday and Monday are closing days, if a holiday comes on a Wednesday, few agents or shops or businesses will reopen just for the Tuesday. That means closure from Saturday evening to Thursday morning. Similarly, a Friday holiday results in an extended closure from Thursday evening to Tuesday morning. May is a particularly bad month, with three or four public holidays (1 May, 8 May, the Feast of the Ascension and, usually, Whit Monday).

Public holidays are observed all over France on the following days: New Year's Day, Easter Monday (but not Good Friday), 1 May, 8 May, Feast of the Ascension, Whit Monday, 14 July, 15 August, 1 November, 11 November, Christmas Day. Local saints' days or other holidays may also interrupt business: check in advance.

Agents will sometimes agree to appointments on public holidays if you seem like a serious buyer. They may also be willing to show you over a house or flat on a Sunday or Monday, but make sure not to abuse this. Remember, too, that many French families entertain on public holidays and Sundays, so don't want visits then.

Don't insist on seeing too many places in a day. It will only confuse you. You should also bear in mind, especially in country districts where distances are liable to be great, that the British residents working for estate agents are generally on a commission-only basis, paying for their own petrol, so it isn't fair to expect them to drive you round all day. You may in fact be asked to contribute to their expenses. Five or six visits in a day should be seen as an absolute maximum.

Do tell the truth about what you are able or willing to pay. Agents report a tendency among British househunters to ask for, say, houses in the region of 700,000 francs, when they don't really want to pay more than 500,000 francs. Beating sellers down is not by any means standard practice in France. You might be able to talk them into taking a few thousand francs off, but to expect a drop of nearly 30 per cent is clearly quite unrealistic, even in a time of recession. What happens, said an agent in the southwest, is that having seen houses at 700,000 francs, clients are inevitably disappointed at what is on offer at 500,000 francs. It is better to start looking at prices lower than you can afford and work up to the right price – then you can feel confident that you're not overpaying.

Do remember that you must allow for legal fees and, in many regions, agent's commission too.

Don't start off thinking that everyone is out to cheat you. Agents report that some clients are so suspicious that it's hard to do business with them. The licensing system means that there are fewer cowboys than in Britain. And the high-pressure techniques often met with in Britain are much rarer in France.

Don't try to get out of paying the agent's commission. It certainly won't make you popular, will reflect badly on your compatriots and may land you in trouble – a seller who encourages you to cheat the agent out of his commission, or falls in with your plans to do so, may not play fair with you either.

One last very important don't: when you have bought your own place, *don't* try to compete on the sly with the local agents by setting yourself up as a middleman acting for British househunters. It won't make you popular in the area and may get you into trouble with the local authorities (see below).

Reading agents' particulars and advertisements

Smaller estate agents and those away from regions attracting large numbers of British buyers are unlikely to provide details in English. Even if you speak French, you will need to be aware of the types of property available in France and how they will be described. Otherwise you can easily waste time visiting something quite unsuitable.

Houses in towns and villages

Houses in a town (*ville*), a small town/large village (*bourg*) or a village (*village*) may be referred to simply as a **maison** (house), but there are a number of variants on the basic term. A **maison de maître**, literally a 'gentleman's residence', is an imposing house, of the type often referred to as 'the big house' in an English village, probably a couple of centuries old. A **maison bourgeoise** is similar, perhaps a bit less grand, and more likely to be nineteenth century. It will often be the equivalent of a solid Victorian family house.

An **hôtel particulier** is not a hotel but an elegant town house or mansion, usually free-standing, sometimes best translated (especially in Paris) as a palace. But the term **particulier** by itself means something less grand. Used in Tours (where it is officially a **particulier tourangeau**), Poitiers and sometimes in Bordeaux and other towns in western France, it is similar to an English terraced family house: tall and built right on to the street, with a small enclosed garden at the back. (Insurance companies may quaintly refer to it as a **maison à touche-touche**, because it touches the houses on either side).

A **villa** is a detached house, usually modern, although it may be late nineteenth or early twentieth century, surrounded by a garden; it is found on the outskirts of towns and villages and in suburbs, and by the sea, where it is the equivalent of an English 'seaside villa'. A **pavillon** is a small detached house, on the outskirts of a town or village, or occasionally in an isolated site in the country; generally modern, but again possibly late nineteenth or early twentieth century.

In the country

In country districts the range is wide, from a modest cottage to a turreted château. A **maison de campagne** simply means a house in the country, not anything like as grand as the picture conjured up by the English term 'country house'. And although the word *chaumière* is the dictionary translation of 'cottage', and is sometimes used as a name for would-be rustic restaurants, it is rarely seen in property advertisements, except possibly for a small thatched house (a *toit de chaumes* is a thatched roof).

At the bottom end of the price scale is the ubiquitous **fermette**, literally a 'small farm' but estate agents' jargon for a small herdsman's cottage, often all by itself in the middle of fields or meadows. It may be pretty from the outside and will often be a couple of centuries old, but unless it has been modernised recently (in which case it will no longer be inexpensive), it will be very basic, little more than an empty shell. It will probably consist of just one room where the family may have shared their living quarters with their farm animals, perhaps with a small room or alcove leading off it used for sleeping. There may be a stone sink (possibly a fairly elaborate one in the southwest, where it is called a *souillarde*) and a small bread oven or cupboard inside the fireplace. There will probably be no running water or electricity and certainly no mains drainage. If it does have plumbing and wiring they will be rudimentary and will almost certainly need replacing. It may well be overrun by rats and mice.

The estate agent may rhapsodise over the potential of its *grenier(s) aménageable(s)* or convertible attic(s). And they may indeed look like the perfect place for putting in extra bedrooms with their tree-like rafters and beams. But beware summer heat and winter cold: unless you are prepared to spend a lot of money on insulation, which will involve taking the roof off and spending several thousand pounds, they will be unlivable in for much of the year. Moreover, they have probably been built with gaps between the tiles to let in light and create a cooling draught in summer – take that away and the whole house will become like an oven.

Estate agents, with the usual optimism of their kind, will tell you that these cottages, which may be on the market for under 200,000 francs, require only about the same spending on them again. But you will need to spend more than that if you want to turn them into even an occasional holiday home. On the other hand, they do offer unlimited opportunities for creative conversion, and at least you won't have to spend time and money undoing someone else's taste. (See Chapter 5 for some sample costs for the type of work you will have to embark on if you buy an unconverted *fermette*.)

A larger house, attractive but not grand, with one or two interesting period features, may be described as a **maison de caractère** or 'house of character'. In some regions, especially the southwest, it may have a *pigeon-nier*, a pigeon tower or dovecot, in the form of a rectangular tower with a pointed roof, usually attached to the house but occasionally freestanding. And it may also have at least one outbuilding, perhaps stables.

We then come to a whole range of rather grand houses. The word **château** covers anything from a full-scale castle (technically a **château-fort**) to a small manor house. It may be the archetypal beautiful seventeenth- or eighteenth-century house, with elegant shuttered windows and a terrace – the sort of place everyone dreams of owning in France. But it may also be a massive nineteenth-century pile – or even a modern replica.

A true manor house is a **manoir** or a **gentilhommière**, often pretty, generally with several outbuildings. A **demeure** is a grand country house, generally surrounded by grounds. And a **domaine**, as readers of *Le Grand Meaulnes* will know, is a whole country estate, perhaps the equivalent of a 'stately home'. A **presbytère**, presbytery or vicarage, may be quite grand, or simply a largish house. And a **chartreuse** is probably a full-scale monastery, though it is also used to mean simply a secluded country house.

A **moulin** is often a charming watermill, in a lovely setting over a river (beware flooding though!), but may also be a windmill that can be turned into an interesting but inevitably small house. A **pavillon** (or **maison**) **de chasse** is a hunting lodge on the edge of a forest, which can be quite elegant if it had royal or aristocratic owners.

Some buildings are typical of specific regions of France. In the Ardèche you may come across a **magnanerie**, a silkworm farm – a rambling farm-house, once surrounded by mulberry trees, with a large space under the roof where the silkworms were reared and wove the silk. A **mas** is a Provençal farmhouse and the Touraine and Anjou have some **maisons troglodytes** or **troglodytiques**, literally 'cave-dwellers' houses', built into the cliff face beside the Loire: some of these are very modest, others quite elegant, with elaborate architectural detail and even little gardens in front. A **maison à colombages** is a half-timbered building, typical of pretty Norman farmhouses surrounded by apple orchards, and of both town and country houses in Alsace.

Outbuildings

Many of these country houses will have one or more outbuildings, known collectively as **dépendances**. They can often be converted into extra family living accommodation or guest cottages. British families often plan to let them to pay for the running costs of the main house, or to cover their mortgage repayments, but this may not be as easy as it sounds (see Chapter 7).

The most common extra building is a **grange** (barn), called a **grangette** if it is really small. **Etables** and **écuries** are stables and a **porcherie** is a building with pigsties. A free-standing dovecot or **pigeonnier**, rectangular in the southwest, probably cylindrical elsewhere, may be thrown in; and so, in the southwest, may a much smaller cylindrical structure called a **garriotte**, originally used as a herdsman's shelter. *Garriottes* have been successfully converted into shower rooms for guests by some families. In Provence you may come across a beehive-shaped **borie**, which served a similar purpose, in the middle of a field. A **buanderie**, wash house, perhaps with its huge copper still intact, may also be free-standing. A **four à pain**, baking oven, may be large enough to be converted.

Situation

Retiré means quiet and secluded, while **isolé** really is isolated – probably miles from anywhere and possibly with no proper access road. **Près commerces** means near shops (though not necessarily actually in a village) and a house **dans un hameau** is one of a tiny cluster of houses, perhaps not more than two or three, officially designated a 'hamlet'. **Vue imprenable** means that you can see for miles – but there is no guarantee that the view will be attractive. **Site boisé** means surrounded by trees, generally in a wood or forest. **Bord de mer** is at the seaside, not necessarily right on the sea.

Flats

The vocabulary for flats is much less varied. An **appartement** is an ordinary flat, **a studio** a one-roomed flat or bedsitter, a **duplex** or **triplex** a maisonette on two or three floors. The word **loft** has become chic for a flat of the artist's studio type or converted from a warehouse, as in New York. An **appartement bourgeois** is a spacious, probably nineteenth-century flat, usually with a separate **chambre de bonne** or servant's room on the top floor of the building; precisely because the traditional owners of such flats had servants, the kitchen may well be poky and dark. An **appartement de standing**, or **grand standing**, is a luxury flat, usually modern.

Buying a château

'Even at the top end of the market, prices are still behind those in Britain.' Philip Hawkes* and his wife Patricia have been estate agents in France since 1976, and since 1986 have had their own business, specialising in historic houses – châteaux, manor houses, country estates and Paris flats – some of them listed buildings. For about five million francs they can show you a 'nice, small and well-maintained eighteenth-century château with ten hectares of land'. The price of a château can go up to 20 million francs, or even 50 million for a very large and beautiful place close to Paris. Even then, as the Hawkeses point out, the price is a great deal less than the cost of construction on that scale.

For three million francs you can buy an attractive small manor house or priory in a pleasant setting. And the Hawkeses' neat folders, full of colour prints, reveal a range of beautiful houses all over the country at prices that really do seem reasonable even by today's standards in Britain. You should, however, expect to have to do some work on them. On the whole houses of this type are not as well maintained as their equivalent in Britain, because their French owners have used them as summer and holiday residences, with a town house as their main establishment. For instance, there may well be no viable central heating. But such houses clearly repay careful restoration, and the Hawkeses may be able to recommend a specialist firm to help you, such as Casa Antica* in the southwest.

Buying a mountain chalet

Chalets, and flats in chalets or blocks, in mountain resorts are popular with British ski, climbing and walking enthusiasts, but also make a good investment as letting potential is excellent. Zigi Davenport of Alpine Apartments Agency* says that by letting for just three weeks in the high skiing season you should be able to cover all your running costs for the year. The ski season in the French Alps lasts for about four months and the high summer season for two months, with June and September also popular for Scandinavian holidaymakers and walkers.

The chic international resorts like Megève, Meribel, Courchevel and Val d'Isère are naturally expensive. So are Annecy, and lakeside chalets or villas. But you can find more reasonable chalets in resorts like Morzine or Samoens, a year-round resort. Prices here range from 450,000 francs for chalets needing modernization to 2 million francs for beautiful upmarket chalets or renovated farmhouses. There are even a few barns and traditional village houses to renovate, from about 400,000 francs. New chalets in traditional style start at about 550,000 and go up to 4 million francs. Studio flats in modern chalet-style apartment buildings tend to be very small but ingeniously designed to make maximum use of space. A typical price is 350,000 to 450,000 francs, but you can find the occasional tiny one for under 200,000.

Having your home built

Alpine Apartments Agency* also specializes in selling plots for those who prefer to have their own custom-built chalet. Plot prices range from 250,000 to 800,000 francs and come with outline planning permission for traditional chalet designs. The agency works with a local firm selling a range of designs from 2 bedrooms to 6/7 bedrooms. You can decide on the internal layout. Prices start at around 500,000 francs, rising to over 1 million.

Traditional designs are also the speciality of the British company Maison individuelle*, who sells completed houses in a range of 150 attractive regional designs in the south-west. It can have the house built on your own plot, or help you find a suitable plot. Prices for 3-bedroomed houses, including fitted kitchens, carpets and floor tiles, start at about 450,000 francs, including 1000 square metres (¼ acre) of land. Two-bedroomed houses start at 300,000. Planning permission is dealt with for you, and so are water and electricity contracts.

Through notaires

Notaires still play quite a large part in the property selling market, especially in country districts. They are often asked to seek a buyer by the heirs of someone whose estate they are handling, and many families remain true to the tradition of asking a *notaire* to perform this role in other circumstances too, in spite of the recent proliferation of estate agents.

You will see property advertised by *notaires* in local newspapers and you may also encounter boards outside houses directing you to the *étude* of *Maître* so-and-so. If you respond to one of these advertisements you will have to pay a fee to the *notaire* for negotiating the deal as well as the standard legal fees. Alternatively you could look up some local *notaires* in the Yellow Pages of the local telephone directory, or ask the Chambre départementale des notaires* for names, and then approach them to ask if they have anything suitable on offer. If they have not had to go to the expense of advertising, and simply put you in touch with, say, the heirs of one of their clients, they may not charge a negotiating fee.

Do not expect *notaires* to provide the same sort of service as estate agents, whose commission is usually higher. They certainly won't be willing to arrange electricity or water contracts for you, or be able to put you in touch with builders.

Through a British intermediary in France

A number of British owners of property in France, having been through the hoops themselves, decided to set themselves up as informal property seekers for their compatriots. You will see advertisements from such people in the British press and in specialist magazines. The idea is tempting: someone who speaks your language, who knows the area, who can give you tips about how to go about buying and perhaps renovating property. But there can be dangers. Their experience of the procedure will probably be limited to their own purchases and a few others, but, as I have pointed out, there can be many variations on the standard theme. They will certainly not be popular with the local agents: the estate agents' federation is trying to stamp out this practice by alerting the authorities to those operating, not only without a licence, but without being registered as a trader (an essential requirement in France). A major clamp-down has resulted, and some offenders have even gone to prison. If it is known that you have been seeing properties with one of these 'clandestine' agents – word goes round quickly, especially in the country – you may well meet a frosty reception if you later approach a full-scale agent. And your intermediary may suddenly have to back out if the local tax, VAT and other authorities start inquiring too closely into his/her activities.

It may be helpful to know that when I was preparing this book, I faxed some of the people advertising this type of service, saying I was writing a book and would like to talk to them about what they could offer my readers – but none of them responded.

I must stress that I am not talking here about British people working on an official basis with French or British agents, who are often a great help to househunters.

Newspapers and magazines in France

Among national dailies, *Le Figaro* is traditionally the place to look for property advertisements. The daily *International Herald Tribune*, published in English in Paris, carries mostly private advertisements for property both in Paris and elsewhere in France.

France has a number of flourishing regional dailies with large circulations. *Nice Matin*, which has several different editions covering individual geographical areas, is a good source of property on the Côte d'Azur and in Provence. *Ouest France* covers Brittany and the Atlantic Coast. *La Nouvelle République* covers the central Loire Valley region. *La Voix du Nord* is the local daily for the Pas de Calais and Picardie areas, and *Paris–Normandie* covers Normandy. In eastern France, *Les Dernières Nouvelles d'Alsace* is the best-known daily.

Don't forget the freesheets published in virtually all areas, with many property advertisements.

De Particulier à Particulier is a well-known specialist weekly covering the whole country and featuring only small ads from private individuals, some of them accompanied by black and white photographs. It is published on Thursday and is very widely available. *La Semaine immobilière* (still often known by its earlier title *Locations et ventes*) has both private and agency advertisements. Both are fat large-format non-glossy magazines with newsprint paper and newspaper layout. *De Particulier à Particulier*, which has a supplement covering new property in new developments, offers its advertisers the possibility of featuring in *The Times's* property columns once a month. Both these weeklies are also a useful source of holiday lets if you decide to stay in your chosen region first to make sure it is right for you.

Belles demeures, a monthly specialising in upmarket properties, is available to subscribers abroad (580 francs for a year's subscription in 1993); write to *Belles Demeures*, 37 boulevard Exelmans, 75016 Paris, France.

Hunting on screen

If you have friends living in France you can househunt on their Minitel, France's teletext system, available to most telephone subscribers. The subscriber television channel Canal Plus has occasional programmes offering 'armchair visits' of available properties; details usually feature on Minitel for several weeks.

Using the grapevine

Those same friends in France may, of course, be able to help you househunt. And it is certainly worth asking around among local British communities to see if anyone knows of a suitable property for you.

Through a British agent

Until the late eighties there were only a handful of estate agents in Britain with French properties on their books. The demand for both holiday homes and permanent homes in France led to a proliferation of agencies specialising in this market. Some were old-established agencies who had turned to this field recently, perhaps to compensate for a slump in the British property market. Others were set up specially with an eye to the growing interest in France.

The recession has in some ways been beneficial to house-hunters, as it has resulted in a shake-out in which some of the less professional agencies have had to close down, while the serious operators have remained in business. Moreover the remaining agencies have seen the wisdom of collaborating. For instance in 1993 **Groupe France** was formed, bringing together seven agencies pledging to maintain high standards and to ensure that if one member cannot produce what you are looking for, or does not cover your area, you will be passed on to another member.

Some agents cover most of the country, like the old-established Rutherfords,* who have specialised in the French market since 1963, originally had mostly country properties but can now offer both old and new houses and flats over much of France. French Associates* have been going almost as long and operate in many areas. Others started up over the last decade prefer to restrict themselves to a few regions. Spratley & Co* focus on new property in the Pas de Calais and in both old and new property on the Côte d'Azur and in southwest France. Barbers,* whose French division started operating in 1985, cover quite a lot of the country but specialise in rural areas, with a good selection of places in Burgundy, a popular area that is not generally well served by British agents.

Some of the more recent agencies also specialise. For instance, Northern France Properties,* as the name suggests, concentrate on the northern strip: from Calais westwards through Normandy and into Brittany as far as Saint-Brieuc, none of them more than two hours from a Channel port. In 1992 they set up Western France Properties,* covering the Vendée, Charente and Lot-et-Garonne. Also self-explanatory is Alpine Apartments Agency*, while French mortgage specialists Crabb & Templeton* specialize in finding commercial property or places suitable for turning into, say, hotels, restaurants or bed-and-breakfast businesses, as well as what they refer to as 'leisure property'.

I have listed some companies specialising in France at the end of this chapter, but have no space to provide a comprehensive picture. You will find others by looking at property columns in the national press and in specialist property magazines or by attending property exhibitions (see below). Unless you have been given a personal recommendation, your choice must be guided by factors such as length of experience in the area, since a year or so is clearly a minimum needed to build up a good network of contacts with French agents.

Splitting the commission

British agents cannot legally sell property in France themselves unless they have their own French agency, which very few do. They must therefore work with licensed French agents. The larger ones have a wide network of contacts with whom they collaborate regularly. Some employ freelance representatives to liaise between their clients and French agents.

Beware of any agent who appears to be selling French property without collaborating with a French agent: the French authorities have reinforced the laws on trading in France and have taken some British operators to court, even when they are based in Britain.

The agent's commission is shared between the British and French agent, on a 50/50 or sometimes 40/60 basis, so you should not be paying any more by buying through a British agent. However it is not always easy to tell, as some agents quote inclusive prices. You should first check whether this means including both the agent's commission (if the buyer pays in that region) and legal costs, or only one or the other.

Some articles in the British press have revealed that property advertised by British agents is sometimes on offer at lower prices in France. And the disadvantage of all-in prices is clearly that you don't know how much commission you are paying and to whom. You should certainly ask about this. The advantage is that you know exactly where you are financially, as well as being able to start the operation at home, without travelling to France. It is up to you to decide whether you are prepared to run the risk of paying a little more in exchange for the convenience of all-in prices. If you aren't, you must ask the agent to break down the price, and if necessary take your custom elsewhere.

Many agents now quote only franc prices, though some use sterling. Again the advantage of sterling is that you know where you stand. But remember that because of currency fluctuations, either the agents have allowed a margin to cover themselves, or the price may have changed by the time you come to buy. Yet others quote franc prices with an approximate sterling price in brackets, as a guideline only.

Back-up services

As the agent's commission on French property is higher than on property in Britain, agents specialising in the French market offer a number of free back-up services that you would not expect from an agent through whom you buy at home. And in an increasingly competitive market, these back-up services are becoming more comprehensive, with some agents offering free legal and other advice where they used to make a charge.

Help with making travel arrangements is common. You may be offered inspection trips, too, perhaps with advantageous rates for ferry crossings, charter flights or full travel-plus-accommodation packages. Assistance with the paperwork involved in a property purchase will normally be provided: from vetting a preliminary contract to arranging a mortgage; organising a power of attorney; liaising with the French agent and *notaire* to ensure that parcels of land and individual properties are accurately described; advising on insurance cover; and recommending legal and financial advisers where appropriate. Mortgage finance and insurance can often be arranged for you, and some agents can also give you the names of surveyors operating in France. Some will also help with arranging electricity and other services or with letting.

Video presentations
Some British agents have produced videos introducing the regions in which they specialise and showing the types of property available. They may include details of a selection of houses and flats currently on their books too. For instance Barbers* have a 1¼-hour video with details of a hundred properties for £11.99 including post and packing.

Other intermediaries in Britain
Property 'brokers'
David Rosslyn-Smith and Sarah Francis of Sifex* like to describe themselves as 'property brokers' rather than estate agents. Their service is popular with busy professional people for whom time is a very precious commodity and who appreciate the 'qualifying' done at the outset. This is David Rosslyn-Smith's term for the process whereby he asks a lot of questions to find out what type of property and which region will really suit his clients' requirements. 'Nine times out of ten,' says Sarah, 'it will be something completely different from what they'd originally envisaged.' Once the priorities have been sorted out, Sifex contact one of the network of French agents with whom they work, mainly in the south-west, and also in the south, and 'deliver them into his or her hands', arranging for them to be met at the airport if appropriate and shown over suitable properties. Since 1988, Sarah says, she has been 'selling the dream and the rendezvous, but after that we're there to negotiate the best possible price'. The company provides a great deal of initial information on the different regions and ways of getting there, and will put clients in touch with mortgage experts and financial and legal advisers as necessary. The properties they find for their clients range from a 300,000-franc *fermette* in the Gers to a 40 million-franc villa on the Côte d'Azur. They also specialize in finding houses with vineyards.

Going through this type of operation will not add to your costs: like conventional estate agents, they split their commission with the French agent. But you can also retain their services to find a specific property, in which case an extra charge may be made.

Property searchers

For those who like the idea of a very personal service, a property 'searcher' is a solution to be considered. Such people work closely with French agents, often specialising initially in one region but subsequently widening their network of contacts as the clients who approach them, as the result of advertisements or word of mouth, ask them to expand their area of operations.

Property searchers act for buyers, helping them to find a house or flat, and working with French estate agents who are primarily acting on behalf of the sellers. Like a British agent, they split the commission with the French agent, but can also undertake a personal search to find a specific property, or accompany you on such a search. They will normally charge a set fee for a personal search, and you may have to pay their expenses, but both fee and expenses will generally be reimbursed if you buy one of the places they come up with. Look out for advertisements from such people in the specialist press.

Legal advisers

British solicitors' practices offering French services, such as those listed in Chapter 3, usually have good contacts with French *notaires* and may be able to suggest property available through them. Some, like Prettys* French Property Finding Service, can offer all the back-up provided by British estate agents, including dealing with electricity and other contracts.

British newspapers and magazines

The property columns of the *Daily Telegraph*, *Sunday Times*, *European* and *Financial Times* carry a fair number of advertisements for French properties and ancillary services. Weeklies like the *Spectator* traditionally have small ads from British people selling and letting French properties, and *The Times* now has a special arrangement with the main French magazine for private advertisers.

But there are also several specialist property magazines now available in Britain, some of them sold in newsagents' and station or airport bookstalls, others by subscription only.

If you cannot find the following magazines in your local newsagent's, write, fax or ring for a subscription leaflet:

French Property Buyer
South Bank House
Black Prince Road
London SE1 7SJ

tel: 071-793 0700
fax: 071-582 4272
Glossy, every two months; features and news snippets, plus advertisements for property to buy or rent and classified ads. @ £2/25 francs per issue, in 1993, £12 for year's subscription.

French Property News
2a Lambton Road
Raynes Park
London SW20 0LR
tel: 081-944 5500
fax: 081-944 5293
Monthly, broadsheet format; packed with short articles on topics of interest to buyers and owners of property in France, news updates and advertisements from agents, private sellers, and a host of ancillary services (surveyors, removal firms, interior and garden designers, solicitors, financial advisers and the like); also runs popular French Property Exhibitions in January and September (see page 83); free for first six months.

Le Magazine
74 Elms Crescent
London SW4 8QX
tel: 071-622 3975
fax: 071-987 2383
Glossy French lifestyle magazine, published every two months, carries property advertisements among much other material; £2 per issue, £12.50 for annual UK subscription in 1993 (£16 rest of Europe).

Living France
France Properties Ltd
9 High Street South
Olney
Bucks MK46 4AA
tel: Bedford (0234) 711 013
fax: Bedford (0234) 240 272
Glossy, ten issues a year; includes features and lists of properties, with colour photographs, grouped by region and covering much of the country; £2.50 per issue; £25 for annual UK subscription (£30 rest of Europe).

France Magazine, the glossy quarterly for Francophiles, also carries some property advertisements and publishes occasional features on property in specific regions. £3 per issue, £14 for UK annual subscription (£17 rest of Europe). For subscriptions: France Magazine, Dormer House, Stow-on-the-Wold, Glos GL54 1BN, tel: Cotswold (0451) 31398, fax: Cotswold (0451) 30869.

Property exhibitions

Although the plethora of French property exhibitions held all over Britain at the beginning of the nineties has now been cut back, there are still a number of major fixtures, as well as French sections in overseas property shows. The monthly *French Property News* organizes exhibitions in January and September at the Hammersmith Novotel in west London. Another top venue is Harrogate, where French Agenda Exhibitions stages a France and French Property Exhibition in early May. The *Daily Telegraph*'s March exhibition in London was cut back substantially in 1993 and combined with other trade shows.

Deciding how to proceed

If you speak reasonable French, know the region well and have plenty of time at your disposal, it makes sense to go initially direct to a French agent or *notaire*. If you are really confident about your French, you may be able to save money by using the French media to find a private seller.

But if your French is halting or non-existent, you must think hard. You may be lucky enough to come across a good local agency with English-speaking staff, or better still with a resident British person working for them who can hold your hand as necessary and in whom you feel confidence. Then you can let them handle the paperwork, having it vetted by a separate legal adviser. Otherwise it will be very hard to cope with the formalities.

By going through an agent or other intermediary in Britain you may (though not necessarily) pay a little more, but you will have someone to turn to when you find it hard to understand what is going on.

Similarly, if you have many work and other commitments, and therefore cannot spend much time going to France to househunt, going through a British intermediary will save time. You will be able to get advice at the outset about the most suitable region for you, all necessary contacts and appointments will be made, travel can be set up, and a lot of the time-consuming paperwork will be taken off your shoulders.

You might consider a two-stage approach. Try contacting some French agents during an initial visit to the region you have chosen. If you find the right agent and they produce the right place, well and good. If not, start contacting British agents or other intermediaries on your return home.

Some useful addresses in France

Fédération nationale des Agents immobiliers (FNAIM)
129 rue du faubourg Saint-Honoré
75008 Paris
tel: (010-33-1) 44-20-77-60

Dubuc Immobilier
Six offices covering Normandy and the Pas de Calais, in Abbeville, Buchy, Dieppe, Eu, Gisors, Neufchâtel-en-Bray

Contact address:
4 rue de la Halle
1 Grande-Rue-Fausse-Porte
76270 Neufchâtel-en-Bray
tel: (010-33) 35-93-92-01
fax: (010-33) 35-93-91-80

Philip Hawkes
94 rue du faubourg Saint-Honoré
75008 Paris
tel: (010-33-1) 42-68-11-11
fax: (010-33-1) 47-42-22-26

Ian Purslow Associates
Château de Saint-Maur
32300 Mirande
tel: (010-33) 62 67 61 50
fax: (010-33) 62 67 59 35
Represents Châteaux et Demeures
en Armagnac (châteaux, mansions
and fine country houses in

Gascony) and Rutherfords* in
south-west France.

Lesenéchal Immobilier
12270 Najac
tel: (010-33) 65-29-74-74
fax: (010-33) 65-29-75-92
Based in the Aveyron, but covers
much of the south-west.

Office notarial de Fréjus
BP15
115 rue Montgolfier
83601 Fréjus cedex
tel: (010-33) 94-53-69-90
fax: (010-33) 94-52-34-93

Some British agencies and intermediaries specialising in France

There are too many estate agents handling French properties for a comprehensive list to be feasible. This list, therefore, includes some of the old-established agencies and some newer ones with specialist fields:

Alpine Apartments Agency
Hinton Manor
Eardisland
Leominster
Herefordshire HR6 9BG
tel: 05447 234
fax: 05447 8900
French Alps and Jura from Lake
Geneva to Swiss and Italian
borders; chalets, farmhouses,
commercial properties.

Barbers
427–9 North End Road
London SW6 1NX
tel: 071-381 0112 or 071-385 6666
Rural houses in Brittany,
Normandy, Charente, Burgundy,
south-west and south.

La Collection française
66 High Street
Manton
Marlborough
Wiltshire SN8 4HW

tel: 0672 516266/514402
fax: 0672 514402
Brittany, west, south-west, south-
east, Pyrenees

Cottages in Rural France
Rose Cottage
Church Road
Swanmore
Southampton S03 2PA
tel: 0489 893 677
fax: 0489 891 501
Buildings of character, from
cottages to châteaux, in Burgundy,
Brittany, Normandy, west, south-
west.

Crabb & Templeton
Chapel Plaister
Nr Corsham
Wiltshire SN14 9HZ
tel: 0225 810 531
fax: 0225 811 211
Commercial and leisure property
throughout France.

French Associates
Robertsbridge House
High Street
Robertsbridge
Sussex TN32 5AN
tel: 0580 880 599
fax: 0580 880 076

Latitudes
14 Piper's Green Lane
Edgware
Middlesex HA8 8DG
tel: 081-958 5485
fax: 081-958 6381
Tunnel area, Normandy, Brittany,
south-west, south, including
châteaux and building land.

Maison individuelle
Contract House
27 Hyde Way
Welwyn Garden City
Herts AL7 3UQ
tel: 0707 376 255
fax: 0707 376 250
Modern houses for existing plots,
plus plot-finding service in
Dordogne or south-east.

Northern France Properties
130 Walham Green Court
Moore Park Road
Fulham
London SW6 2DG
tel: 071-386 9826
fax: 071-381 4934
Tunnel area, Normandy, Brittany.

Propriétés Roussillon
Rousillon House
29 Aversley Road
Kings Norton
Birmingham B38 8PD

tel: 021-459 9058
fax: 021-458 1325
Rousillon, but also Languedoc,
rural, coastal and ski resorts.

Rutherfords
25 Vanston Place
London SW6 1AZ
tel: 071-386 7240
fax: 071-386 5122
Rural properties all over country,
Côte d'Azur villas and flats,
commercial, vineyards.

Sifex
Phoenix House
86 Fulham Road
London SW6 3LF
tel: 071-384 1200
fax: 071-384 2001
Property brokers specialising in
south-west and south, plus
vineyards, and châteaux and
manor houses throughout France.

Spratley & Co
60 St Martin's Lane
London WC2N 4JS
tel: 071-240 2445
fax: 071-240 2469
Tunnel area, south-west, Côte
d'Azur.

Western France Properties
130 Walham Green Court
Moore Park Road,
London SW6 2DG
tel: 071-386 0026
fax: 071-381 4934
Vendée, Charente, south-west.

5 RENOVATING YOUR HOME

Since the late eighties many thousands of British families have bought rural buildings needing extensive restoration in France, particularly in the north and southwest. Many of these modest, and not so modest, cottages and farmhouses, barns and village houses, have a great deal of charm and can be turned into delightful holiday homes. But agents report that, unlike the pioneers who have been slowly doing up tumbledown places for years, some of the more recent buyers haven't fully appreciated how much needs to be done and have had a shock both at the expense and at the time involved. Many such places have no mains water, drainage or electricity. You need to spend quite a lot before they are even habitable, let alone really comfortable. When I was preparing this book I heard many stories of people who had still not been able to use their new French home at all, nine months or so after completing the purchase. No doubt because of such stories, an increasing number of people have opted for places that have been at least partly restored and modernised, and can therefore be used for holidays straight away. Of course they are more expensive, but not necessarily more expensive than if you bought the same type of place with everything needing doing and did it up to the same standard.

The point of this chapter is not to put you off restoring a charming country building, but to help you understand what is involved and to give you some pointers about how to proceed. To ensure that having rhapsodised over the view, thankfully not disfigured by hideous pylons, you come down to earth and realise that the old-fashioned-looking light switches do not necessarily mean that the house is now connected up – and that the cost of being reconnected may be pretty hefty. If there has been no electricity in the building in recent times, you may have to pay about 10,000 francs per pole. You may also have to pay for bringing the telephone to your hamlet.

If there is no mains drainage, you will have to install a septic tank or *fosse septique*, a term that tends to loom large in the life of British people with holiday homes in rural France. It will cost more to install on rocky terrain. To bury gas tanks in the ground for central heating and other uses will cost up to 6000 francs. You obviously need enough land to be able to put in both septic and gas tanks. If you need 100 metres of water piping to connect your house, it will cost about 5500 francs, including installing a water meter.

As a rough rule of thumb, you can expect to have to spend at least 350,000 francs to make a two-storey building with about 60 square metres per floor (plus cellar and attics) habitable as a holiday home. That is the same again as it would have cost you in the first place, excluding up to another 20 per cent on legal and mortgage fees, plus agent's commission.

To turn it into a home that can be lived in year-round would cost a great deal more. Expect to spend a minimum of 4,000 francs per square metre to bring up to a basic habitable standard a semi-ruined house with two floors of 60 square metres each, costing 150,000 francs excluding legal and agency costs. That means 450,000 to 550,000 francs on renovation to a minimum standard.

David Marr Limited,* working in the southwest, have kindly provided detailed figures for some of the work you may need to undertake. Prices do not vary as much as you might expect from one part of the country to another, as trade associations have recommended scales of charges for their members. In 1993, for instance, 120 francs per hour + VAT seemed to be the average hourly rate for a skilled craftsman working on country properties.

Some sample prices for renovation and restoration
Figures supplied by David Marr Limited*, including VAT

Roofing
removing and re-laying canal tiles, replacing
    broken tiles where necessary, clipping tiles on
    to the roof (but not replacing main structural
    woodwork)   FF290 per sq metre
repointing copings   FF152 per sq metre
finishing cornices (canal tiles)   FF85 per sq metre

Insulating
supplying and installing 180 mm thickness glass
    fibre insulation   FF66 per sq metre

Septic tank (*fosse septique*)
installing a 3,000-litre tank (complete)   FF27,500
supplement for installation on rocky terrain   FF5,000 approx

Bathroom
supplying and installing (all in white): bath,
    lavatory, bidet, washbasin, shower including
    80 x 80 cubicle, all connections, taps and
    evacuations   FF15,500

Kitchen
installation costs on a kitchen costing FF35,000   FF3,500 approx

Attic
putting two rooms into attic, properly finished
    and insulated   FF170,000 approx

Swimming pool
installing a 12 x 6 metre pool in rocky terrain, with
   60 sq metres of terracing   FF155,000

Renovating a three-bed farmhouse to a high standard (all work by registered builders and craftsmen, with ten-year guarantee)
   demolishing internal structure (four days' work)
   installing seven dormer windows
   installing two French windows
   replumbing
   rewiring
   carpentry throughout
   new staircase
   new *fosse septique* (3,000 litres)
   installing bathroom and shower room
   installing new fully fitted kitchen with all appliances (washing machine,
      fridge, dishwasher, oven and hob)
   ceramic tiling in kitchen, bathroom and shower room
   floor tiling in one room
   painting and decorating throughout
   installing electric heating and hot water system
   installing washbasins in two bedrooms
   finishing out and insulating roof space
   new lighting
   installing in-ground gas tanks
   installing 10 x 5 metre swimming pool with 60 sq metres of terracing
   carpeting upstairs
TOTAL COST (including furnishings and equipment)   FF 705,000

Renovating a similar three-bed farmhouse to basic standard:
   building costs only, excluding work on the roof,
      without furnishings or appliances   approx FF 315,000

Be VAT conscious!
Don't be tempted to take on unregistered workmen to save the VAT you'll
otherwise have to pay. Local inspectors have the right to visit building sites
and houses being renovated to check up on this and you will get off on a
bad footing if you start breaking the rules before you have even moved
properly into your new home.

    Also, you must keep proper receipts (which inevitably means including
VAT) for all work done on your house, to mitigate the effects of capital
gains tax when you eventually sell the place (see Chapter 8).

How much restoration?
If you are doing up a holiday home, I strongly advise you to put a ceiling on
what you intend to spend on renovation and restoration. There will always

be more you could do, but you should concentrate on getting the key items dealt with, then sit back and enjoy the place without feeling you've overspent. You can gradually do more over the years, taking one job at a time so as not to be too out of pocket.

If you are going to live there permanently, you must proceed differently. You must get it comfortable enough to live in year-round, and clean and modern so that you can fill it with your furniture and belongings. But even then, don't set your sights too high at first. Of course you must always get estimates before giving the go-ahead, but it is easy to get carried away and find that you are running out of funds.

Talking to the locals

If you have fallen in love with a house, it is always tempting to close your eyes to potential problems and persuade yourself that if it has been standing for two or three hundred years, it isn't likely to collapse now. But it is wise to check that there haven't been any recent changes that might alter the position.

One British family, who thought just this about a slightly rickety-looking outbuilding they planned to turn into a little overspill for friends who came to stay, were dismayed to find that it had become an unsalvageable ruin during their first winter absence. They subsequently discovered that shortly before they had first viewed the place, the owner had sold some of the outbuilding's roof tiles in a separate deal.

It had rained heavily that winter. With half the tiles gone, the rain rotted the wood, the beams became weak, the stone shifted in the gales – and their pretty little guesthouse was little more than a heap of stones. It would have been so expensive to rescue it that they had to abandon the scheme entirely.

The moral of that story is: ask around. And if you discover that something similar has taken place, make sure you do the necessary patching up before the winter.

A typical conversion

A small unconverted house in the countryside typically consists of a large kitchen with open fireplace, a largish bedroom and a tiny room used as a storeroom, with an attic upstairs used for storing grain. A typical conversion turns the kitchen into a living room with a small kitchen area, divides the bedroom into two, and puts a shower room into the little storeroom. If the climate is suitable, the attic can be insulated and converted into extra bedrooms.

Obtaining planning permission

Local planning regulations are set out in the *Plan d'occupation des sols*, generally known as *POS*. You should work on the principle that any new building, and any change to the outside of an existing building, require planning permission (*permis de construire*). So does the installation of a septic tank. If you want to demolish all or part of a building, the term is *permis de démolir*. Applications must be made to the local *mairie* and may take some months to come through. Planning controls are strictly applied in France and you will soon be in trouble with the local authorities if you do not comply. This may also apply to some internal alterations, like demolishing a staircase – always check before embarking on substantial internal renovations. If you have failed to obtain planning permission you may face severe penalties, as well as being ordered to restore the place to its original condition.

Stephen Smith of Prettys* warns against assuming that if a neighbour, or an acquaintance in a nearby village, has obtained planning permission for, say, an extension, you can go ahead with similar work before being sure that you too will be granted permission. The regulations (*règles d'urbanisme*) vary from one region and one *commune* to another, and as no two buildings are identical, the same criteria may not apply. If there is a substantial amount of land attached to the building, it may be wise to consult a lawyer.

As in Britain, there is normally a set period (typically a couple of months) during which the public is entitled to appeal against planning consent.

If your new home is in a listed area (*site inscrit*), or all or part of it is listed as a 'historical monument', expect the process to take longer still (see Chapter 3). De Pinna, Scorers and John Venn* warn that 'defacing a historical monument' can be considered a criminal offence. In a listed area, you may be told what colour you are allowed to paint your shutters or what additive to use. Even in a non-listed area, use of materials may be the subject of controls. For instance, if you are demolishing a shed with a tiled roof, you may not be allowed to use the tiles for a kitchen extension, because current regulations in that area insist that even buildings not visible from the street must have slate roofs.

David Marr Limited* warn that while local officials are usually helpful, they do not respond well if you become aggressive, or even try bribing them with bottles of whisky, as some British people do! If you behave politely and the alteration is quite minor and straightforward, permission may take only a matter of days. They add that the main criterion is that any modifications should preserve the integrity of the building.

When in Rome . . .

The most crucial piece of advice must be: do as the locals do. For a start, if you want to become part of the local community, even for only a short time every year, you must fit in with local ways of doing things. Even where specific regulations don't prevent your doing so, you certainly won't win many friends by putting up a prefabricated breezeblock structure in your garden or grounds. Although the French are on the whole less vehement about conservation than the British, you will win respect by *your* respect for local styles of architecture and decoration.

Anyway, there's usually a good reason for local ways of doing things. I thought the glass and wrought-iron canopies over front and back doors in the Touraine a petit-bourgeois affectation until I realised that in the Garden of France, with its abundant rainfall, it made sense to protect the doors from the worst of the rain – and it was good to have some protection yourself when you were unlocking your front door or signing for a registered letter or chatting to your neighbour across the way. And having planned to get rid of what seemed to me a dangerous metal bar outside the French windows in my study, just waiting to trip me up, I soon changed my mind when I was told that when the rain drove in from the west, as it often did during summer storms, it would come flooding in under the tightest-fitting doors and windows.

Then again, you may wonder why terraces in southern country districts are covered with dull grey paving stones when prettily shaped terracotta tiles would look so much more attractive. But, as many people discovered in Britain in the exceptionally hot summer of 1989, tiles buckle and crack in high temperatures and soon have to be replaced. And although you may much prefer the look of stripped pine shutters, neatly varnished, remember that because of the (literally) blistering summer sun, you'll need to put on a new coat of varnish every year. The locals' use of thick paint in dark colours may be less to your taste, but it will mean a lot less work – and will also look more authentic. Drive round the countryside looking for this sort of detail and you won't go far wrong.

For instance, you may notice that farm gates in the area all have a little wooden roof over them. Without it, torrential rain and gales followed by fierce sun will wreak havoc: the sun on the wet timber dries it out too fast and it splits. If you replace a gate or build a new one, copy the local practice. Centuries-old traditions usually have a practical reason behind them. Don't be afraid to ask the locals about such things. They'll generally be delighted to tell you about them. And ask their advice on matters like what to burn in your fireplace. They'll know what will burn best in the local conditions and will save you from unsuccessful experiments.

Before you replace little windows with huge bays, think about summer heat. It's easy to be snooty about the locals lurking indoors and pulling the shutters across as soon as the sun comes out. But once you've experienced the fierce heat of the July sun on the Mediterranean coast, or even more in a dry inland region like the Ardèche, the Drôme or the Lot, you'll understand their attitude. You obviously want to enjoy being out of doors, so plan two eating areas, with two separate tables: one for the milder morning sun and for evening drinks and meals on the terrace, one for the heat of the day – preferably beneath a tree. And follow the tradition of putting up bead curtains to keep the flies out.

Dealing with builders, workmen and craftsmen

The first point to be aware of is that jobbing builders have never been common in France. In areas where large numbers of foreigners have congregated, they have started to make an appearance, but elsewhere the French method is to deal separately with all the various workmen and craftsmen. This means that if you are completely restoring or renovating a house, you will probably have to find, negotiate with and supervise the work of a large number of different people: mason, roofer/tiler, carpenter, plasterer, plumber, electrician, painter/decorator, glazier and so on. The plumber may have a mate and the mason will probably have a team of labourers, but many of the others will be one-man businesses, with their wives doing the paperwork on an elderly typewriter. It is a time-consuming business dealing with so many different estimates, bills – and people, most of whom are bound to come running to you at some point complaining that one of the others is behind schedule. You will often have to exercise your powers of diplomacy.

Taking on a supervisor

Such supervision is certainly very difficult indeed if you're not on the spot. It may therefore make sense to look for someone to take on the job for you. If you have used an architect he/she may well be helpful about finding specialist craftsmen, but will rarely be the best person to coordinate them and organise and supervise their work in detail. More suitable will be a superior foreman, called a *maître d'oeuvre*, or a rather grander *conducteur de travaux*, who will brief the men where necessary and check that everything is done correctly and on schedule.

Another alternative, especially if you do not speak good French, is to use the services of one of the British people resident in France who are experienced in this type of work, such as David Marr Limited*, to whom I have already referred. Some French and British agents are also able to help in this direction. For instance, Charentes Property Search,* a Franco-British agency specialising in the Charente and surrounding areas, have set up a restoration service for their clients. As with surveyors, you can look out for advertisements for such people, taking up references to be on the safe side.

Using British builders

Advertisements for British builders operating in France are also common in the specialist press. Some are resident in areas like the Dordogne with a large British community. Others are based in Britain but specialise in travelling over with a team of workmen to do the job for you. Or you may think of bringing over a builder whom you have used in Britain, putting him and his men up in your house or in caravans on the site.

The obvious advantage of doing away with language problems may make this seem an attractive proposition. But you should think very carefully before doing so. Firstly, and perhaps most importantly, you will not endear yourself to the local community. Hostility to the British buying property is very rare in France, not least because we have a reputation for doing up tumbledown buildings with taste and sensitivity. But it may well appear if too much British labour is imported. Presumably you are planning to buy in France because you like the country and the French way of life. So it would be foolish to make the path to integration sticky by alienating local opinion. You may also find the local authorities less cooperative over matters like planning permission if you never use local labour. And the neighbours may well be less willing to keep an eye on the place in your absence.

You should also consider that local craftsmen are familiar with local climatic conditions and with local materials and building techniques. They are fully aware of local building regulations, know where to lay their hands on whatever materials you need to complete a restoration in keeping with the character of the area, and will be able to call on extra skilled help as required.

Moreover – and this is the second important point – standards of workmanship are very high in France. The apprenticeship system is alive and well and pride in work is not, as it sadly so often seems to be in Britain, a thing of the past. You would be hard put to find British workmen able to match the quality of, say, local masons or joiners. Indeed, one problem may be that because there are so many skilled craftsmen, it may be difficult to find ordinary labourers to do the unskilled jobs! Then again, all building work must bear a ten-year guarantee, with two-year guarantees on small jobs – a plus point well worth taking advantage of.

It must also be said that some new British property-owners have discovered to their cost that some of the builders moving out from Britain have left failed businesses behind them and are merely seeking a cushy life in the sun.

If you do use British builders, it is essential to make sure that they have full accident insurance cover. An E111 will not cover work accidents, nor will an ordinary holiday insurance policy.

Potential problems

Most British people using French tradesmen and craftsmen are delighted with the quality of their workmanship. But there are two slight drawbacks.

The first is that you will find it hard to persuade them to cut corners. As a result you may have to spend more than you had planned on doing up a house that may after all be used for only a month a year. But in the long run you will undoubtedly be so pleased with the result that you will forget the cost – and the restoration will certainly call forth the admiration of your British friends.

The second is the other side of the coin of skilled workmanship and a determination to do the job properly by sticking to the rules and observing local customs: you may find workmen inflexible when it comes to departing from what they see as the norm.

Let me give an example. I once had great difficulty in persuading the plumber and carpenter working on my kitchen that I really did want the sink placed higher than the 'standard' height from the ground. I am tall by

French standards and I have a bad back, so the last thing I wanted was to be hunched over. As it was a brand-new kitchen, I said, surely I could have it at any height I wanted? 'But *Madame*,' they said firmly, 'that's how it's done here.'

Eventually I solved the problem by summoning a site meeting at which I towered over not only the electrician and the plumber, but the stone-mason, the plasterer and the painter too. When I gently pointed this out – I didn't want to offend their male pride – and demonstrated how far I would need to bend over to use the sink, they saw my point and rather sheepishly agreed.

A similar battle occurred when I wanted a washbasin across a corner in the bathroom, with a triangular tiled area behind it. Again I was told it 'wasn't done'. I eventually won that one too – and later had the satisfaction of overhearing the *conducteur de travaux* boasting of his 'innovatory solution to a space problem' when he showed a potential new client over the house to admire his team's work.

I should add here that in provincial France, at any rate, women master-minding operations may encounter some resistance from local workmen. As a woman – and a foreigner to boot – I was treated to many a condescending remark on the lines of my not needing to bother my pretty head about the technical details when I tried to get across what I wanted. I soon noticed, too, that all estimates and bills went to my husband, even though it was I who discussed the work to be done. In the end I swallowed my feminist pride and asked my husband to intervene. Hc got all the various men together: 'My wife and I have paid for this house jointly and she is just as much your client as I am. Anything she asks you to do is to be considered as coming from both of us.' After that I had no more problems and I recommend the method. You may rebel against having to do it, but British pragmatism should win the day.

Another area where you are liable to meet resistance is in electrical installations. French electricians seemingly never cease to be amazed at the number of power points their British clients ask for: the French are used to having adaptors and flexes running all over the place. And if you are having a dishwasher and a washing machine installed, you must make it clear that you may want to use both at once. Otherwise you may find that you have a single outlet pipe for both. (See Chapter 6 for a warning about making sure you have enough power to be able to run both.)

A few tips

If you're doing up a rambling farm building don't get carried away by all those vast acres of space, probably much more than you're used to at home. Yes, Provençal tiles would undoubtedly look superb on the floors of the kitchen and the huge new living room you've created with its lovely old stone fireplace. But you'll be amazed at how the bills mount up.

- The French are fond of using fabric (*tentures murales*) rather than paint for walls, even in the country. As so often, if you're using French workmen you may do well to follow local custom. A big advantage is that you can have a thick underlayer (*molleton*) which provides both insulation and soundproofing. But beware of foam underlays, which may not be fireproof. They are also liable, if you have central heating, to dry out and crumble, then drop down and cause a lumpy ridge at the bottom, spoiling the hang of the fabric. The specialist shops where you can choose the fabric and the braiding that is traditionally used to edge it should be able to put it up for you if you don't want to do it yourself.

- Roller shutters in PVC – good for insulation and security – can be ordered in colours that blend with the stonework or brickwork for back doors. They let the light filter through, too, in the same way as traditional wooden shutters.

- French plumbers are liable to be obsessed with being able to get at their pipes and you'll have a hard job persuading them to hide them away behind the walls. The French don't seem to mind seeing pipes running down walls, even in elegant drawing rooms, and they are rarely worried by visible electricity cables either. You can have it all boxed in (*coffré*) by a carpenter – at a price.

- Exposed beams are an attractive feature of old houses: they add cachet and are often singled out in estate agents' descriptions. But they can cause problems. If you don't want dust and sawdust falling into your food and covering all your possessions, you'll have to sand them down and creosote them. This is a job best done by professional sandblasters.

- As I pointed out in Chapter 4, think carefully before embarking on converting attics into living rooms and bedrooms. If you haven't already visited the area at all times of year, do some homework on high summer and winter temperatures. And see whether other people in the area have been able to make satisfactory conversions. If you do decide to go ahead you will probably have to take the roof tiles or slates off first, then put in insulation. This will probably cost at least 30,000 francs.

- In old houses, particularly those with just such attic rooms – once probably used as grain stores – you will almost certainly have a problem with rats and mice. If you are not there year-round, the chances of getting rid of them permanently are slim. Lower your sights and concentrate on keeping them out of the areas where you most don't want them to be.

- Don't panic about woodworm! Many British people do, but these rural buildings have sturdy oak beams and woodworm can never penetrate as far as the heart of the oak.

- *Fosses septiques* involve a delicate ecological balance, which you mustn't do anything to disturb. It is essential not to use any chemicals and to stick to cleaning products that are stated to be suitable for *fosses septiques* (though modern all-water systems are less sensitive). Tampax and sanitary towels must never be flushed down the lavatory, a fact you must impress on guests and tenants, unless you have a modern system that will, allegedly, take anything – check carefully, and err on the side of caution. The tank may need cleaning out about every seven to ten years if the house is being used as a holiday home – a job for professionals. Again, some modern systems will not need this major clean.

Electrical appliances
White goods are more expensive in France than in Britain. It is nevertheless advisable to buy fridge, dishwasher and washing machine on the spot: because of power differences, any machine you take over probably won't work so satisfactorily, and you will have difficulty in getting it repaired or serviced unless it is a French make.

The same goes for small apparatus like plate warmers, microwaves or toasters: they may heat up more slowly, especially if you have a low-kilowatt supply (see Chapter 6).

Your best bet is to watch out for the special bargain weeks or months staged by household appliance stores, when prices will be considerably reduced. Your neighbours or the estate agent should be able to tell you where you can get the best prices.

Useful addresses

Casa Antica
24130 La Force
tel: (010-33) 53-57-32-58
Specialises in restoring, renovating and decorating châteaux and fine old houses in southwestern France, including those in very poor condition. Works for France's Historic Buildings Commission.

Charentes Property Search
16230 Saint-Angeau
France
tel: (010-33) 45-39-22-98
fax: (010-33) 45-39-24-48

David Marr Limited
Jambes
82160 Pulyagarde
France
tel: (010-33) 63-65-71-41
fax: (010-33) 63-65-72-04

Maisons Paysannes de France
3bis rue Léo-Delibes
75116 Paris
An association dedicated to preserving traditional rural dwellings and farm buildings and rural sites; can give advice to those restoring such places, and publishes both a quarterly magazine and a series of useful booklets (in French) on specific aspects of restoration; has representatives in most *départements*.

6 BEING A HOMEOWNER IN FRANCE

'The first qualification is to have a love of France. It doesn't matter if you don't speak French, as long as you're prepared to have a go.' A British journalist and teacher living in the southwest and working with an estate agent dealing with British clients was giving her recipe for making a success of having a home in France. It's a good recipe, and it remains valid whether you have bought a holiday home or are going to live there permanently.

You won't enjoy your French home if you don't fit in with the local community. To do so, you must be willing to talk to people, however halting your French. Forget any impression of unfriendliness you may have picked up from trips to Paris – Parisians are indeed often unfriendly – or from condescending waiters in crowded Mediterranean resorts. In the rest of the country, and especially in rural areas, you'll generally find a genuine warmth and lively curiosity that will draw you into the local community. But you must be prepared to make an effort yourself. It's true that provincial cities can seem like closed societies, unwilling to accept outsiders, but even that changes in time; and as soon as you go out into the country, attitudes are quite different.

It's no good coming over with preconceptions about how things work in Britain. Don't get irritated by the differences, but show an interest in why things are different. There's usually a good reason – historical or climatic or because of some local custom or superstition – and it will be endlessly rewarding to talk to the local people to find out such reasons. Ask about local cuisine too – perhaps a recipe for some unfamiliar vegetable you've spotted in the market – and you'll soon break the ice.

Consider taking French lessons during the winter if your French is non-existent or in need of more than brushing up. Your efforts will be appreciated and once you've got a good grounding, it will soon improve as you talk to people.

Attitudes to foreigners
Thanks to a number of rural exoduses at various times during the last couple of hundred years, France has a huge reserve of rural properties that have not been lived in for decades or even centuries. So by buying a country property you will not be driving some young couple out of a home. And because the supply of such properties is nowhere near drying up as yet, you won't be pushing up prices so that they're out of reach of the locals either. Moreover, tax incentives for buying new property, plus the average French person's lack of enthusiasm for doing up a tumbledown building, mean that most local couples will prefer a comfortable modern flat or one of those small modern houses perched up on a little mound with a cellar

and garage beneath that you see on the outskirts of towns and in the countryside all over France.

As a result, you're most unlikely to encounter resentment at the idea of foreigners buying property, old or new. There was extensive media coverage in Britain of the decision by the Mayor of Honfleur to put a stop to foreigners taking over certain parts of the town and its outskirts. His objection was, understandably enough, to having half his patch turned into a holiday village, dead out of season. But he wasn't against the British as such. His reaction, anyway, seems to have been an isolated incident. In researching this book I travelled to many areas and found no instance of resentment at all, provided the newcomers were prepared to fit in and did not emulate the Dutch, who have a reputation for bringing all their supplies with them from Holland, never patronising local shops, restaurants or tradespeople. (For advice on this, see **Shopping**, page 110.)

The local authorities are also pleased to have previously empty houses inhabited, as they can collect a local tax from the newcomers to boost their budgets. (See **Taxation**, page 112.)

Being neighbourly

Dropping in for a chat and a cup of coffee or a drink with your neighbours is not a French habit. But stopping for a gossip on the doorstep or in the baker's or in the market square is, with, of course, the ritual handshake at the beginning and end of the conversation. Start by building up relationships in this way. Join in local events – the village fête or the clay-pigeon shoot or the angling contest in the next village. Go along for a drink at the *mairie* on the Fourteenth of July (Bastille Day and France's National Holiday) and watch the religious procession on Palm Sunday or the Feast of the Assumption or the local saint's day.

That way you'll soon feel part of the community and will be accepted as such, even if you're only around occasionally.

Inviting neighbours in for meals is also not a regular habit in France. But many a British family has been touched by a neighbour appearing with a little earthenware dish brimming over with some local speciality for you to try. You might return the compliment by cooking something very English and taking that round. Or bring some shortbread or fancy biscuits in a pretty tin for them on your next visit, or sweets for the children, or perhaps a Stilton cheese in a traditional pot. Tins with traditional scenes and mugs with pictures of the royal family are usually a hit in the countryside. Do send Christmas cards. They may only respond – if at all – with a formal visiting card, but your gesture will be appreciated.

You may eventually be asked in for a rather formal meal, for which they will clearly have got out the best china and will probably have bought expensive dishes from the *charcuterie* and a cake or tart from the *pâtisserie*. You might have preferred good home cooking, but that's the way it's done. Whereas in Britain it's a compliment to your guests to have taken endless trouble to make everything yourself, the French, who regularly take that sort of trouble with their own family meals, consider it more of a compliment to go out and buy everything. If you pluck up your courage and ask them in for a meal, they'll probably behave very formally, at least the first couple of times.

Using first names between adults probably won't happen for years. French neighbours usually go on calling each other 'Madame' and 'Monsieur' for the rest of their lives. If you try using their first name, they're unlikely to respond in kind, so it's probably better not to start. And certainly don't launch into the familiar '*tu*' instead of '*vous*'. The general rule is: never use '*tu*' to adults unless and until it is used to you. Children and pets are another matter. But even then you can get into difficulties with teenagers: French teenagers tend to look younger than their British counterparts, and, even after living in France for years, I often found myself worrying because I'd used '*tu*' to someone who looked about twelve, but turned out to be sixteen or even eighteen! When in doubt, always use '*vous*'.

One final thing: don't be cliquey if there are other British people in the area. It won't make you popular with the locals.

Doing business

Any sort of transaction will be an opportunity for a leisurely discussion over a glass or two of pastis or local wine. Don't rush things. One agent in Cahors, a Belgian who has lived in France for many years, told me of a negotiation for an extra piece of land that went wrong because he brought up the subject too soon: 'You've got to adapt to local ways of doing things. If not, you'll never get anywhere. But if you're prepared to take things slowly, have quite a lot of friendly sessions in the café first, when you do eventually raise the subject, gradually, everything will probably go fine.' He advised that if you hope to buy a piece of land beyond your own plot, you should wait for months or even years before broaching the subject with the local farmer, until you've got to know him and his family a bit. Otherwise he'll think you're too keen and will hold out in the hope of pushing you into overpaying for it.

Utilities
Electricity

Electricity is supplied by the state-run Electricité de France, known as EDF. Charges are based both on consumption and on the amount of power you have available. Bills are sent every two months, but your meter will be read only every four or six months, or even once a year in country districts. So most of the bills are estimated. If you are using a house as a holiday home you may well find that all your bills are estimated as you are not there when the meter readings are to be taken (flat owners may be able to come to an arrangement with the janitor, or meters may be outside the flat). You can query a bill by supplying your own meter reading just as you would at home. Voltage is 220V, or occasionally still 110V in the country.

It is important to make sure that you have enough power for your needs. The three basic rates are 3 kilowatts, which is described as *ménage* (ordinary domestic supply), 6 kilowatts, described as *confort* (convenience supply), and 9 kilowatts, described as *grand confort* (luxury supply). The *ménage* supply will be adequate if you have no large electrical appliances other than a refrigerator and no electric kettle: it will be enough for ordinary lighting and for small appliances like an iron. *Confort* will enable you to use an electric kettle and either a dishwasher or a washing machine or an electric cooker at any one time. To be able to use two or more of these machines simultaneously you must opt for the most expensive *grand confort* rate.

If you have electric heating you will need to step up the power to a still higher rate – at least 12 kilowatts. And a pool will probably mean you need even more power. You can go up to 36 kilowatts. Beware of the high cost of electric heaters and the likelihood that you won't be able to use them all at the same time.

You should be able to change from one rate to another if you find you have made the wrong choice or if you acquire new appliances. But again you should check this locally.

If you overload the system, a trip switch (*disjoncteur*) will operate. It is as well to check where the switch is as soon as you settle into your flat or house and have a torch in some easily accessible place, especially when you're cooking. I have vivid memories of having to warn dinner guests in one flat in Paris that we might be plunged into darkness during the *apéritif*: if a boost was needed to get my electric oven back to the required heat, and another couple of rings were switched on, the lights might well suddenly go out and a sound like a pistol shot would indicate that the trip switch had leapt into action. Whereupon I would reach for my torch, switch off one of the rings and make for the switch to salvage the evening. Remember that if you have bought a house, the switch may well be in the cellar.

Saving on bills

Electricity is generally more expensive in France than in Britain, but you can economise in various ways. For a start, you can choose between a basic charge rate, which applies at any time of day or night, and a higher rate that enables you to take advantage of cheaper night-time rates (*tarif heures creuses*). Night-time rates apply between 10.30 or 11 p.m. and 6.30 or 7 a.m. depending on the area. You may incidentally find that your lights become a little dimmer when the night-time rate starts.

The second rate is to be preferred if you have, say, a dishwasher, as you can save money by switching it on after 10.30 or 11 p.m. If you opt for this system, you will have two separate dials on your meter, one labelled *HC* or *heures creuses* (and perhaps with a moon on it) and one labelled *HP* or *heures pleines* (and perhaps with a sun on it). Your bill will also distinguish between your daytime and night-time consumption.

If you are sure that you will not be visiting your French home during the coldest winter months, look into the scheme known as EJP. This means that you will pay a lower standing charge than either the basic or double-rate schemes. For 95 per cent of the year, consumption is charged at a low rate (roughly the same as the night-time rate under the double-rate scheme). This is registered on the HN (for *heures normales*) dial on your meter. But for the remaining 5 per cent of the year (twenty-two days), the cost of consumption for eighteen out of the twenty-four hours shoots up to about ten times the HN rate. This high-rate period is not fixed: it depends on the weather, and other local factors, though it always falls between 1 November and 31 March. It is referred to as *heures de pointe mobile* and the dial is labelled PM.

You can get your electrician to put in a light or bell or other warning signal, which will flash or ring or whatever half an hour before a high-rate period begins, so that if you do have to be in France at that point you can make sure to keep your consumption to a minimum. You can also get him to arrange matters so that various pieces of apparatus can't work during the expensive periods. The object of the exercise is of course to encourage you to cut back on consumption when demand is at its peak.

Requesting a supply and paying bills

As so often in France, you will normally have to apply in person at the nearest EDF office and sign a contract specifying the number of kilowatts and the type of charge rate you have chosen. But if you have bought through an agent or have taken on a legal adviser they might be able to deal with this for you. In towns you may be able to make the arrangement by telephone, if you speak French.

If you are setting up a holiday home, paying by direct debit is the sensible method to choose. Don't forget to take along a *relevé d'identité bancaire* (see **Banking**, page 114) or give one to the agent. Otherwise you can pay by post or in person at the EDF office or the post office.

When you check your bill, you may be puzzled by two differing VAT rates: the standard rate is added to the total figure for consumption, but a lower rate applies on the standing charge.

Safety

As a general rule, safety regulations are not as strict as in Britain, though they are becoming stricter. For instance, switches and power points are allowed in bathrooms, although (except for shaver points) they may not be within a certain distance of the bath or shower. And two-pin plugs and sockets without an earth are common, although they are not supposed to be used in kitchens or bathrooms, or in rooms with tiled floors.

If you are buying property that does not need substantial renovation, you would still be well advised to have the wiring checked by a competent electrician. If you are having it rewired, or wired for the first time, make it clear to your electrician that you want switches outside the bathroom and lavatory. Wall switches governing power points are not normal practice in

France. You can solve the problem for, say, an electric kettle, by attaching a plug with a built-in switch.

On the whole it is wiser to buy any electrical apparatus and appliances in France. Anything you take over from Britain is liable not to work so satisfactorily, and repairs will invariably be a problem. One advantage of this: in France, apparatus always comes with plug attached, as it so maddeningly doesn't in Britain

I feel I must mention that I had a bad experience as a result of incorrect wiring in France. Because my electrician had not checked that some previous wiring had been done properly, I received a violent electric shock when I was in the bath and was lucky not to be seriously injured. As it was, I was quite ill for several weeks. It may seem unfair to draw any conclusions from an isolated incident, but I couldn't help noticing that whereas my British friends were horrified, my French friends didn't seem particularly surprised and virtually all said they had had similar experiences themselves.

The moral is: ask around to make sure you use a competent electrician and impress on him that he must check any work done previously. And insist on having enough power points.

One final point: in country districts the electricity supply may fail during thunderstorms. In fact many country people simply switch everything off, and also unplug the telephone, when a storm blows up. Have a gas lamp (and a spare cylinder) handy and keep a stock of candles.

Gas

Mains gas is supplied by the Gaz de France or GDF authority. Charges are based on consumption and, as with electricity, you can select a day/night charge rate if that suits your requirements.

Outside towns it has traditionally been standard practice to use gas in cylinders. You will see rows of them in various sizes outside hardware stores and local depots: check the nearest supplier and always keep a spare cylinder just in case. Even if you prefer cooking on electricity, it is wise to have one gas ring with cylinder attached, of the type used by campers, in case the electricity supply fails. Nowadays, you can have gas tanks (for central heating, say) sunk in the ground outside the house.

Bills for mains gas are sent every two months, but meters are read only every six months or annually. Your bill will probably be on the same sheet as your electricity bill, and will be set out in the same way. For getting yourself a supply (see **Electricity**, page 99) as you can normally see to the necessary formalities for gas and electricity at the same time, via the same EDF/GDF office.

Water

Mains water is supplied by the local *compagnie des eaux*. There is no general water rate: you pay instead according to your consumption. Bills are sent annually or every six months, with payment usually required in two weeks. Again it is preferable to arrange for a direct debit rather than risk postal delays.

If you are restoring a house, you may have to pay a connection charge to the local network (see Chapter 5) and also pay for a meter to be installed. If you plan to add a swimming pool, or to design a garden that will need a lot of watering, make sure you have pipes wide enough to cope with the volume of water.

In the depths of the country, you will probably have to get your water from a local spring (*source*) or well (*puits*). Make absolutely sure that you do have access to a source of water and that none of your neighbours can turn it off unilaterally or use it all up. (Remember *Jean de Florette*?) Even in towns, several pages of the sale deeds of a house may be taken up with stipulations about your having to grant access to the well in your garden to the neighbours, if there is a water shortage.

Water from wells and springs is probably not safe to drink. If you want to check this out, have a sample tested. But even if the result is satisfactory, you will need to have it tested again at regular intervals. Better stick to bottled water to be on the safe side.

Water shortages are rare in towns. But they do happen, and are quite common in country districts during hot summers. You may think it worth installing a storage tank just in case.

Telephones

The French telephone system (France Telecom) is fully automatic and mostly excellent, with sophisticated equipment available. The only thing that may still seem antiquated is the time-consuming process of getting yourself connected, though the situation is improving.

If you are buying new property, or restoring an old house that has never been connected (or whose line was discontinued generations ago), you will obviously need to apply for a new line. But even if you are buying from someone who is on the telephone, you cannot simply take over the line and number from the previous occupant.

In most cases you will need to go in person to the nearest Telecom office (*agence commerciale*). Check the opening times carefully and be prepared for a long wait. While you are waiting, you will have to fill in a form handed to you by the receptionist. This will ask for details of your address, the type of equipment you require, the number of the line already operating (if relevant), the billing address (if different) and the method of payment (again go for direct debit if you are using the place as a second home and take along a *relevé d'identité bancaire*).

A word of warning: if a line is already installed in the house, the previous occupant must request its closure before you make your application. Check with him or her to save yourself a wasted journey, or get your agent to do so. The good news is that if you move within France, the formalities are much simpler the second time round.

Various types of apparatus exist, for rental or purchase. You may also buy a telephone from a private firm, but it is advisable to choose a model that is Telecom-approved (*agréé*). You can apply at the same time for a Minitel (see below), buy an answering machine or fax and ask for various refinements such as having your bills itemised or being ex-directory. All such optional extras have to be paid for. The charge quoted is usually monthly, although bills are sent every two months.

In towns your application will probably be dealt with within a few days. You will be sent your new number through the post, along with the official acceptance of your application and confirmation of costs. If you ask nicely, you may be able to find out the number on the spot. But don't rush to get any cards printed: you will be warned that the number may have to change and only the written confirmation counts. In the country you may have to wait weeks, or even months in remote areas, to be connected. If you are restoring a 'wreck' or building a new house, make sure that you have trenches dug for telephone cables.

Costs

The connection charge for a new line is considerably higher than that for an existing line. While you are in the office, pick up a leaflet showing the current call charges and a colour-coded chart showing when calls are cheaper. Keep it by the telephone to encourage foreign visitors to pay for their calls! At the time of writing, calls to Britain were cheaper between 9.30 p.m. and 8 a.m. on weekdays, on Saturday afternoons and all day Sunday. The system is more complex for calls within France, with calls naturally more expensive during working hours and cheapest at night and at weekends. Times change frequently, so make sure you update your leaflets regularly.

Directories

When your application for a telephone has been accepted, you will be given a voucher (*bon*) for the telephone directory (or directories) for your *département*. You must take it along to the appropriate office (usually in the same building) to collect your directory, either the same day or later. You can choose between two sizes: the larger is about the same format as British directories; the smaller is neater and easier to handle, but the print is very small.

Yellow Pages (*pages jaunes*) exist in France too. They are either bound into the ordinary alphabetical volume or, in regions with many subscribers, printed as a separate volume.

There is no operator service in France. For directory inquiries dial 12. You may be offered the opportunity of having a Minitel, a small monitor and keyboard on which you can access an electronic telephone directory. You can also use it for obtaining a wide variety of useful information (rail and air timetables, your current bank balance, theatre and cinema programmes and so on) and for booking and buying certain items. You can even househunt on it (see Chapter 4). In some parts of France Minitels are supplied free; elsewhere there is a monthly rental charge. If you have children, be careful. The Minitel can be used for all sorts of fun and games (including access to soft porn, incidentally) and children are liable to run up a hefty bill once they get their hands on it.

Faxes and answering machines

Fax machines are now very common in France and you can send faxes from many Telecom offices and from private copyshops and the like. If you need your own, both faxes and answering machines can be bought (not rented) from France Telecom or a private company. Again, go for a model that is *agréé* and don't be tempted because of higher prices in France into trying to take one from Britain: it won't work so satisfactorily because of power differences and repairs will present problems.

A final tip: all French telephone numbers now consist of eight digits. These are invariably expressed in pairs. Thus 47-33-21-58 will be expressed as *quarante-sept, trente-trois, vingt-et-un, cinquante-huit*. It'll take time to get used to it, but you must just plug away at it until it comes naturally. Be particularly careful when taking down a number in the seventies or nineties: when you hear *soixante* you are liable to write down 6, but if the number is, say, *soixante-dix-sept* (77) you will be caught out; and the same applies for, say, *quatre-vingt-dix-huit* (98). For calls to anywhere except Paris and its suburbs, you simply dial the number. To call a Paris subscriber, dial 16, wait for the second tone, then either 1 (for Paris proper) or 3 or 6 for the suburbs. From within the Paris area, to reach a provincial subscriber dial 16 and then the eight-digit number after the tone. For international calls dial 19 (though EC harmonization will eventually change this to 00), followed by the country and area codes and the number.

Postal services

The French postal service is reasonably efficient, although as prone to strikes as its British counterpart. The standard practice of using registered post for all official documents means that you may spend quite a lot of time in the local post office – and so will the rest of the population, so be prepared for a long wait. Stamps can be bought from the tobacco counter in cafés, but supplies are liable to run out, especially during the summer tourist season.

Postcodes are essential nowadays. Get a fat yellow booklet called simply *Code postal* from the post office: it lists postcodes for all *communes* in France, in alphabetical order.

There is no obligation on postmen to deliver right to your front door, unless it is on the street. Otherwise you will have to attach a letter box to your front gate, in one of several regulation formats. In blocks of flats, letters are handed to the *concierge* or *gardien*, who distributes them among the individual letter boxes on the ground floor. Even if your front door is on the street, the postman may insist on your having a bigger letter box cut into it, if you frequently receive large envelopes that don't fit through it.

Registered letters can be signed for only by the person to whom they are addressed. A wife cannot even sign for her husband or vice versa, unless a special document (*procuration*) has been signed at the post office to authorise this (for instance if one has to have a spell in hospital). And concierges and neighbours certainly can't take in registered letters for you (unless you have organized a *procuration* for them). Which is another reason why there are always long queues at the post office, as people collect their registered letters.

Refuse collection

In towns refuse collection operates much more efficiently than in Britain: the dustmen (*éboueurs*) come round every day, and may even appear on a Saturday if the next Monday happens to be a public holiday. Dustbins must be of a regulation format, as they are hoisted automatically into the dustcarts, but they come in various sizes. Everything must go into the bin – do *not* leave plastic bags out. If you have large items to be removed, contact the town hall: you will be told which day has been designated for collecting such refuse in your street (usually once a month). Then put the objects outside, or in the courtyard of a block of flats (check with the janitor first).

In the country things are more complicated. You may still have to make trips to one of the less attractive features of the French countryside – the *décharge publique* or public refuse tip. With a bit of luck your *commune* will by now have splashed out on large bins on wheels grouped together at some strategic point, in which you can place bags of household rubbish. The French are becoming quite environmentally conscious these days and some of the bins may be used for papers and magazines only, or for bottles (bottle banks are becoming common too). In remote places, there may be a rubbish collection service only in July and August: locals and holiday-makers can bring refuse to a fenced-off collection point.

Waste-disposal units

These are virtually unheard of in France. But if your property has mains drainage (*not* if you are the proud owner of a *fosse septique*), there is no reason why you should not take one over from Britain. Don't forget that you will need an appropriately-sized hole in your sink – and be prepared for your plumber thinking the whole project outlandish. I solved the problem by arranging for someone to bring me over a unit along with a stainless-steel sink top already cut. The plumber and electrician grumbled, but installed it perfectly satisfactorily – and were eventually so impressed that they brought along other clients to see it in action.

Security

Unless you have bought a large house and have resident domestic staff, or will have a cleaning lady or gardener coming in from time to time, security can be a worry. But the worry will be considerably lessened if you have slowly built up good relationships with your neighbours and the local community in the way I have suggested. The goat lady passing every day in the country will soon spot anything amiss, the neighbours will be suspicious of callers claiming to be friends of yours. In a block, it is always wise to tell the *concierge* or *gardien* of your comings and goings.

It is still, of course, sensible to have nothing of real value in a place that is not lived in for much of the year. The sort of solid furniture you'll be installing in country districts to withstand the cold and damp of winter shouldn't be particularly attractive to burglars, and wherever your French second home is, it's sensible to steer clear of pretty little objects you'd be sad to lose.

Make sure that you have all the locks and other forms of protection required under your insurance policy – and that you use them as instructed (see Chapter 3).

If you do have a break-in, you must report it to the police and your insurance company within a set time (check with your insurer).

Chimney sweeping

If you have an open fireplace, don't forget that the chimney will need sweeping, especially if you are not using the house over the winter and all sorts of debris may have collected in it. Annual sweeping is advisable, and will probably be one of the co-owners' obligations if you have bought a flat in a condominium. *Ramonage* or chimney sweeping is usually carried out by a roofing contractor (*entreprise de couverture et de zingerie*).

Television and radio

Do not try taking a television set from Britain – it will not work in France because the systems used are different. Unfortunately televisions, like all electrical goods, are more expensive in France. Cable television has caught on in France and satellite television is becoming quite common, but the dishes are likely to be more expensive than at home.

You can keep up with what is going on in Britain by listening to the world service of the BBC or, in many parts of France, to Radio 4 on long wave, though this was under threat at the time of writing. Long-wave reception may be poor on the lower floors of blocks of flats. A few places near the Channel coast can also receive BBC television programmes.

Television licences (*redevances*) are payable annually, although there is no radio licence. It is curiously difficult to *stop* paying a television licence if you sell your French home. As with insurance policies, you remain liable for the licence fee unless you have given official notice that you no longer have a television set in France; and even then you will be asked questions about who now has the set, to ensure that a licence is being paid for it.

Cars

If you are thinking of buying a home in France you presumably know the country as a visitor and will therefore be familiar with the rules and regulations on such matters as priority from the right, carrying a red warning triangle at all times, and so on. If you aren't, you can get information from the AA's Import and Export Section (Fanum House, PO Box 50, Basingstoke, Hants RG21 2ED. tel: Basingstoke (0256 20123) or from the RAC's Travel and Information Services (RAC House, PO Box 100, South Croydon, Surrey CR2 6XW, tel: 081-686 2525).

You may decide that it will make sense to leave a car in France, so that you can make frequent visits to your new French base without a lot of tiring driving. In that case, consider buying a car that runs on diesel: petrol is expensive in France. At the time of writing diesel is considerably cheaper than petrol and also gives you better mileage to the litre. As a result it is widely used, especially in country districts, where distances between villages and hamlets are often great and the roads are winding and therefore slow. You will, of course, have to insure it, and pay the annual road tax, known as the *vignette*, because the round label which is so called must be displayed on your windscreen to prove that your insurance is up to date. You must also register the car in your name and will receive in return a *carte grise* (the equivalent of a log book). Citizens of other EC countries do not need to take a French driving test. Provided they have an EC driving licence, they merely have to exchange it for a French licence within twelve months of possessing the French car or of moving to France permanently; the requirement that you must pay to have it translated has now been abolished, though in some country districts the message has been slow getting through.

Thanks to the Single Market, importing a car into France is now relatively easy. If you are taking over what is deemed to be a second-hand car (i.e. one you have been driving in Britain for at least three months) and are an EC citizen, there are not only no customs controls but no VAT to pay either. If you decide to buy a new car in Britain before leaving, do it within three months of your departure and you will not have to pay VAT or road tax when you buy it, but you must pay VAT when you get to France (the period can be more than three months if you drive it for less than 3000 kilometres before reaching France). As the Single Market is giving birth to many changes at the time of writing, double-check the situation when you are ready to move.

On the other hand, you should consider whether as a permanent French resident you would not be better with a right-hand drive car bought in France.

Cars kept permanently in France, and therefore registered there, bear number plates identifying their owners' *département*: the *département* postal code forms part of the number plate. It follows that if you move your French home to another *département*, you will be issued with new number plates and registration documents. You must anyway report a change of address to the *mairie* or *préfecture* (*Service des cartes-grises*) within three months of moving, even if you stay within the same *département*. If you sell your car in France you will have to supply the same office with the name and address of the new owner.

Pets

Only pets over three months old may be taken into France. If you want to take in more than three pets, you need special permission from the Agriculture Ministry. Before leaving you must ask your vet for a certificate for each pet stating that it is in good health and has had a recent anti-rabies vaccination, and carry with you both the certificate(s) and a translation into French. Although customs controls no longer exist for citizens of other EC countries, you may still be asked by the relevant veterinary official to produce the certificate when you arrive in France, or at some point in the future. When you first consult a local French vet he or she will also want to check that all is in order. Best make several copies to be on the safe side.

Don't forget that if you are only on a short visit, your pet will have to go into quarantine when you return to Britain.

Dog licences are not required in France, but you must register your dog. Ask at the local *mairie*. It is normal practice to take out insurance cover in case your dog bites someone, causes a road accident or otherwise becomes a danger to life and limb. You should be able to add this to the household insurance policy you take out for your property and possessions.

In most French parks and public gardens you will find signs saying that dogs must be kept on a lead. Fines are imposed on those who persist in ignoring this ruling.

Employing domestic help

Employing, say, a cleaning lady or a gardener, even for only a couple of hours a week, is not nearly as straightforward as you might think. *Travail au noir* (literally 'black' labour, i.e. unregistered labour, with no tax paid and no Social Security payments made) is considered a serious offence in France, and is likely to get the employer into as much trouble with the authorities as the employee. So do not be tempted into taking on anyone without doing the proper paperwork.

You will have to give the employee a completed weekly pay slip, including the complex payments you must make (and calculate yourself) for Social Security, unemployment, sickness and holiday pay and so on. And each quarter you must fill in a forbidding form to be sent to the appropriate authority.

As you will probably be taking someone on at the recommendation of a neighbour or other local person, ask them about hourly rates (there is a statutory minimum) and the various percentages for your contributions to the Social Security system. You must then register as an employer with the local URSSAF office. If nobody local can help you, go to the office in person to complete the necessary papers and ask for advice. Provided you are polite – don't rail against French bureaucracy, however exasperated you feel – the officials will usually be quite helpful, especially in country districts.

Shopping

Shopping hours essentially fit in with local living patterns, with the long lunch break respected in provincial towns and country districts, and by many shops even in large towns. This means that food shops are open roughly from 8.30 a.m. to 12.30 p.m. and again from about 3.30 p.m. or 4 p.m. to 7 p.m. or even 8 p.m. Many are open on Sunday mornings but shut all day on Monday. Bakers may open as early as 7 a.m. Non-food shops in the provinces typically open from 9 a.m. to 12 noon and 2 p.m. to 7 p.m., Tuesday to Saturday, and may also open on Monday afternoons. In provincial towns department stores may not close at lunchtime and some supermarkets also stay open all day.

There has been a mushroom growth of *hypermarchés* or superstores on the outskirts of towns. Although you may find these useful, you will find it easier to make friends in the local community if you patronise the local shops. Even the smallest villages will have either a bakery or a *dépôt de pain* – perhaps the local café or newsagent's – to which freshly baked bread is delivered daily. Small local greengrocers, butchers or fishmongers may charge more (at least on some items) than the supermarket, but you will be getting good fresh local produce and can enjoy chatting to the shopkeepers and locals and improving your French – which is rarely the case with the checkout girl in the supermarket! In country districts you should ask around to see which local farmers and smallholders are willing to sell eggs and poultry or fruit and vegetables. And you may well find that the newsagent's or café has the occasional box of strawberry punnets or local mushrooms in season, brought in by a customer or by the café or shop owner himself.

Then there are the *marchands ambulants* who drive round the countryside selling meat or fish or groceries or dairy products, or a mixture of all of them, from small vans with built-in counters. Ask around to find out which day or days they call on and keep an ear open for the horn sounding to warn of their arrival. Some mainly operate from a fixed place in a village – say, beside the post office – but others drive right to the door of their regular customers, even in remote hamlets.

Markets

Many of these 'lorry shops', as my nephews christened them, are also to be found at the local market. Shopping in colourful openair food markets is one of the greatest pleasures of the French way of life for many British people with homes in France. You will soon get to know the little old ladies who bring in fruit and vegetables from their gardens, or delicious goat's milk cheeses, and become friendly with the people who run the butcher's and fish stalls. Joining the local populace on market days, and having a coffee or a drink in the market square once you've finished your shopping, is one of the best ways of feeling that you're taking part in the life of your chosen town or village.

You'll soon find out which day or days are market days – and where you can park to avoid the crowds. Markets are such a magnet that in the depths of the countryside the bank and the insurance office may open only on market day, and the sleepiest little towns suddenly spring into life up until lunchtime, when most markets close. Sunday markets are particularly good if you're looking for bargains: perishable goods are often marked down drastically as closing time draws near (local regulations are strict about markets shutting on time).

Also worth exploring are the covered markets in towns, most of which also open in the afternoons. To find them, ask for *les halles*.

Furnishing your home

Buying furniture and small items like lamps for your home can be a big disappointment. Many a British family has harboured dreams of rummaging in junk shops to find pieces in local woods and designs, only to find that junk shops are virtually non-existent. Serious antique shops can be found in most towns, and in villages in tourist-frequented areas, but the prices tend to be very fancy. And a sign saying *Antiquités* in the countryside is likely to direct you towards a courtyard full of mediocre and overpriced pieces that have little local character. When you do find an attractive piece, it is liable to be in poor condition (watch out for heavy staining to disguise defects).

I have occasionally been lucky at a fleamarket (*marché aux puces*) held in the open air. Many provincial towns hold them at frequent intervals, sometimes weekly (usually at weekends). The equivalents of our Victorian bits and pieces have never become fashionable in provincial France, so you may be able to pick up a bargain along these lines.

If you're not tied to the school holidays for your furniture expeditions, you may find what you're looking for in the local auction room (*salle des ventes*). In the summer season it may be shut, or it will be overrun by wealthy Parisians pushing the prices sky-high.

Another alternative is to seek out local craftsmen, but even if you're buying without a middleman, you may be shocked by the prices. Craft fairs, generally held in the tourist season, are fun to visit, but again prices are generally high.

You may eventually have to abandon your dreams and visit the furniture superstore outside the nearest town.

Remember, anyway, that if you're going to be leaving your furniture throughout the winter in an unheated house, it must be very sturdy to stand up to the cold and the wet. You don't want to come back next summer and find that it's all warped.

Local transport

Bus services within towns are usually adequate, but generally do not operate after about 8 p.m., except in very large towns, where a couple of lines may run in the evening. Even in Paris, most bus routes are not served after 8.30 or 9 p.m.

Country bus timetables are geared to two main categories of passengers: people going into the nearest big town to shop or work in the morning and returning in the late morning or evening; and schoolchildren. As a result, services are likely to be most frequent on market days and during term time. Some services close down for the whole of the school holidays (which means a large part of the summer).

Links between rail and local bus services are usually good. If friends come to visit you by train, you will probably be able to advise them of a train that is met by your local bus, and pick them up at the bus stop, rather than having to drive miles to the nearest station.

Leisure activities

Many towns and even villages have built swimming pools recently. And tennis courts are becoming more common (but remember that the summer heat, probably much greater than you are used to at home, restricts playing to the early morning and evening). They may be open for only a few months a year.

During the summer holiday season travelling circuses and even openair cinemas may visit the most out-of-the-way villages. Each *commune* has its *fête*, when the feast day of the local saint is celebrated in various ways, ranging from a *vin d'honneur* in the *mairie* (which it would be churlish not to attend) to a lively hop in the parish hall with a local band. Clay-pigeon shoots, oddly known as *ball-trap*, are a fixture in country districts – join in the fun and you will soon be accepted as part of the community.

But remember that over the winter months many villages and hamlets virtually shut down. The weather can be pretty bleak, even in the south, people only go out when they have to, and only basic food shops are open. This can come as a shock if you have previously only known the area in the spring or summer, and is one of the many reasons why it is important to visit it at different times of year before committing yourself to a purchase.

Taxation
Personal taxation

As a non-resident property owner in France, the personal taxes that may concern you are income tax, value-added tax, wealth tax, capital gains tax and inheritance tax. You will also be liable for various local taxes.

If you have any doubts about your status as a non-resident, for instance because you intend to spend several months a year in France, or will be doing some of your work from there, you *must* take expert advice on the subject from your accountant and from a tax specialist familiar with the regulations in both France and Britain.

National taxes

Non-residents are obliged to make an annual return for French **income tax** (*impôt sur le revenu*) if they receive income from letting property or from providing bed-and-breakfast accommodation (see Chapter 7).

You will soon become used to paying *TVA* (*taxe à la valeur ajoutée*), the French equivalent of **VAT**. But you may also be called on to register for VAT yourself if you are letting furnished property (see Chapter 7).

Wealth tax, now grandly called *impôt de solidarité sur les fortunes*, is payable by non-residents whose French assets are worth more than 4.39 million francs (1993 threshold – the figure is adjusted on 1 January every year). So if you are thinking of buying a house worth that or more, check how much you will be liable for. The tax applies to the assets of the whole household and includes furniture, jewelry, works of art, yachts and the like as well as property. In 1993 the tax started at 0.5 per cent and rose to a maximum of 1.5 per cent on assets worth 42.5 million francs and over.

Capital gains tax (*impôt sur les plus-values*) may be payable when you sell property in France (see Chapter 8).

Inheritance tax (*droits de succession*) is payable by each person who inherits French property or a share in it. The rate is dependent on how close your relationship is to the person who has died and, unlike the situation in Britain, spouses are not exempt (see Chapter 3).

Tax-resident status

If you become a French resident for tax purposes (which does not necessarily mean that you live there year-round) you will be liable to income tax on your worldwide income, and to wealth tax on your worldwide assets. This is a complex issue that must be handled by an expert. Once you are ready to consider such a step, take your expert's advice about the most favourable time to make your change of residence, and about making sure that you benefit from all the allowances to which you are entitled.

There is no PAYE system in France: everyone is expected to fill in their own tax return and get it into their local tax office by the end of February. Don't be late! Fines are levied for late completion and may be payable even if there is no tax liability. Interest will also be charged if you pay late. Any tax due is paid either in three instalments, or monthly by direct debit.

Ordinary French citizens, unless they are very wealthy, rarely use personal accountants to handle their income tax. But as a foreign resident you would certainly be well advised to use the services of an international tax expert, at least until you have been living in France for some time and are thoroughly familiar with the system.

You must also check carefully on your tax situation in Britain. A double-taxation treaty between Britain and France normally means that you will not be taxed twice. But make absolutely sure that you do not have to pay on both sides of the Channel.

Local taxes

There are two standard local taxes payable in France, roughly equivalent to the rates in pre-council tax Britain. Both are based on the property's theoretical rental value, adjusted every year in line with inflation. As with most French taxes, fines are imposed on those who fail to pay by the required date.

The **taxe d'habitation** is payable by the occupier of the property, who need not necessarily be the owner. It is due annually from whoever was the occupier on 1 January in the year in question. This does not mean whoever was physically in residence on 1 January: you still count as the occupier even if you only use the place for summer holidays. But it does mean that there is no apportionment between buyer and seller, as there used to be under the rates system in Britain. If you become the occupier on 2 January or later, you will not have to pay anything for that year at all.

Those over sixty for whom the property is their *main* residence are normally exempt. You should also be able to claim exemption if you have bought a property but, because it needs renovating, will not be using it straight away and therefore have not moved furniture in. But you will, of course, have to go to the *mairie* to point this out and ask for an exemption.

The second tax is the **taxe foncière**, a land tax which is payable by the owner of a property, whether or not he or she lives there. It is often paid in one lump sum by whoever was the owner on 1 January; but unlike the *taxe d'habitation*, apportionment may be made between buyer and seller nowadays. If there is to be apportionment, this should be stated in the preliminary contract of sale.

Taxe foncière is payable even on a piece of land that is not built on. It may be divided into two parts, one for the building and some of the land surrounding it, the other for the rest of the land. There are exemptions for some agricultural land, and for the first two years after a new property has been built or substantial restoration has been carried out. In any case, this is not normally a particularly onerous tax.

If you have bought property in a popular tourist area you may have to pay a third form of local or regional tax, designed to cover the extra costs incurred in providing tourist amenities. (A small sum for the same purpose may be added to hotel bills in the area, so that the burden is shared between holidaymakers and local owners.) If the vendor and agent are not forthcoming on this topic, you can check with the local *mairie* whether or not it applies to your area; and if it does, how much you will have to pay.

Company taxes

If you have bought French property via a company (see Chapter 1), other taxes such as corporation tax may be payable. Such taxes are frequently modified, so you need expert and up-to-date advice.

Banking

Bank opening hours vary from town to town and from region to region. In country districts and many provincial towns banks are shut on Monday but open on Saturday. In large towns and in Paris they are open Monday to Friday. In small towns and villages in rural areas the only bank may be open only on market day. Opening hours are typically 9 a.m. to 12 noon and 2 p.m. to 4.30 or 5 p.m., but in large towns some of the banks will probably stay open at lunchtime (although their exchange counter may well close for lunch).

You may wish to have an account with a French branch of your British bank. The advantages of this are that you are sure to find staff who speak English – probably the top management will be British – and that transfers from one account to the other will be relatively straightforward. But only the largest British banks have French branches offering full facilities to private account holders, and these branches are not found outside Paris or large towns with resident British communities. In my experience, they do not encourage you to use them for private current accounts: for instance, they may insist on a fairly large sum being kept in the account at all times (not an attractive proposition when it is not earning interest).

You will anyway need a local bank for everyday purposes. The choice will obviously be a personal one, but it may be useful to know that the Crédit Agricole is the most widely represented bank in country districts, with altogether over 10,000 branches in France and over 12,000 cash dispensers.

In French banks you do not normally deal with the manager (*directeur*), but with the person who has been assigned to your account. When you open an account you will be given a card telling you the account number and the name of the *responsable*, the person whom you should contact if you have any queries or problems. It is a good idea to build up a relationship with this person, so that you can telephone him or her whenever you need to, even when you are back in Britain. French banks are not known for the speed with which they answer letters and you will find this personal contact invaluable.

Opening an account

You will need to show your passport and to provide your address in Britain. Accounts can be opened in joint names if you wish. The main advantage of doing so will become sadly apparent if one of you dies suddenly: a joint account will continue, whereas an individual account is generally frozen immediately after a death, causing problems to a spouse or other relatives.

Current accounts

You will obviously need a current account (*compte chèques*), for which you will be issued with a cheque book (*carnet de chèques* or *chéquier*). It is currently illegal to pay interest on current accounts in France, although with the advent of the Single Market, there have been some moves, initially by foreign banks operating in France, to have the regulations altered to allow greater flexibility. It may take as long as three weeks to get a cheque book the first time, and at least a week for subsequent ones, so make sure to order in plenty of time. You have a choice of types of cheque book: most banks offer them *sans talon* (with no stubs), *avec talon simple* (with a stub of the kind you are used to in Britain) and *avec talon correspondance* (with an ordinary stub and a separate tear-off section that you can complete and send with the cheque for the recipient's files). Standard cheque books consist of twenty cheques, but the cheque book request slip enables you to request fatter cheque books with fifty cheques if that suits you better.

The slip also asks you to state whether you want the bank to keep the new cheque book for you (it will do so for up to a month) or to send it to you. Think carefully about this: cheque books are always sent by registered post and must therefore be signed for. This may cause complications, as in France only the person or persons to whom a registered envelope is addressed may sign for it (see **Postal Services**, above). You can also ask for the cheque book to be handed by the bank to a third party named by you on the slip.

Important! It is illegal in France to be overdrawn. A bounced cheque is considered a serious matter and, with even more stringent legislation now in force, might, if you do not provide the necessary funds quickly, result in your being forbidden to hold a cheque book for as long as ten years, and even to operate any other form of account. Remember that with postal delays between France and Britain you might not be aware that a cheque has bounced until after the deadline for topping up your account has passed. It also takes a surprisingly long time for cheques to clear, unless they are drawn on banks in the same town or area. So it is sensible to keep rather more in your current account than you would at home, just to be on the safe side.

This situation explains why cheque cards do not exist and why you are rarely asked for any form of identification when you pay by cheque. If you are asked for identification, show your passport. You will also need to show your passport if you are withdrawing money from a branch other than the one that holds your account.

Nowadays you do not need to write a cheque to withdraw cash in many branches. Simply show your passport and the details of your account on your cheque book: the computer system will be used to check that your account is in funds, and you will simply sign a receipt for the money.

If you want to make payments by direct debit for services such as electricity, you will need to send the authority a slip giving details of your account (*relevé d'identité bancaire* or *RIB*). You will receive one of these at the front of each new cheque book and can request as many more as you like. It will also be useful if you are to receive money direct from a French source: again, send the slip to whoever is to make the payment.

'Putting a stop' on a cheque is possible in France only if the cheque has been lost or stolen. You will receive a dusty answer if you try to stop a cheque because the goods for which it paid were faulty.

Deposit accounts
The bank will be able to suggest various forms of interest-bearing accounts. The standard equivalent of a British deposit account is called a

compte sur livret. Check your tax position in relation to interest received on it.

Loans for property buying

Banks are the standard source of finance for property buying. (See Chapters 1 and 3.)

Credit cards

Major British credit cards will often be accepted in France. The French, once reticent in using credit cards, are now enthusiastic profferers of plastic, and even small restaurants in country districts usually take them. As a general rule, a Visa card is the most widely accepted, and can also be used in some cash dispensers.

As you are affected by the exchange rate when you use a British card (it may have moved against sterling when the time comes for you to pay your bill), you may prefer to use a card issued in France, which will also come in useful for withdrawing cash from dispensers all over the country. Any payments you make by credit card are debited automatically from your account at the end of the month. You therefore do not have to write a cheque each month. Payments made will be listed on a separate sheet that comes with your statements and should be queried if there appears to be an error.

An annual fee is normally charged for holding a credit card. You can choose between a national card (for use only in France) and an international one. You will probably not think it worth paying the higher fee for the international one unless you are planning to move to France permanently: you can use your British card for payments outside France.

Dealing with a death

Sudden death can happen at any time, and there is little worse than having to deal with the formalities in a strange country, especially if you don't speak the language.

Under French law, deaths must be registered at the local *mairie* or town hall within twenty-four hours. You will need to take along a death certificate signed by a registered doctor. Unlike the practice in Britain, this does not refer to the cause of death, which is considered to be a confidential matter. If the death is sudden, the coroner (*médecin légiste*) will have to come round and check that nothing untoward has occurred.

If you are faced with this situation, it is likely that you will want the body to be returned to Britain for burial or cremation. This is a much simpler matter than you might expect. As the British consul said to me when I unfortunately had to cope with a death, with so many people travelling abroad, and road and other accidents relatively common, transporting coffins is now a routine procedure for airlines. The easiest way is to arrange for someone in your family to contact a local firm of undertakers in Britain and check with them what paperwork is needed at the other end, then put them in touch with the French undertakers, who are appointed by the *mairie*. The funeral directors (*pompes funèbres*) will probably have an office at the *mairie*, where you can choose the coffin and complete any necessary formalities. Do not expect the kindly manner traditionally adopted by British undertakers: their French counterparts are civil servants and tend to hide behind bureaucracy rather than showing human warmth.

As no cause of death is given on the certificate, you may need a separate statement from the doctor that the death was not due to a contagious disease, to satisfy airline regulations.

Dealing with a birth

Births can also occur unexpectedly. They must be registered, again at the *mairie*, within three working days, even if the parents are not permanently resident in France. You will need a birth certificate signed by the doctor or midwife.

Don't worry about nationality: children born in France of non-French parents do not automatically become French. But it would be as well to register the birth with the nearest British consulate, in case of difficulties later on – especially if you may possibly take up residence in France at some later date. When you get back home you can apply to have the child registered as a British citizen during the twelve months following the happy event.

Useful addresses

British Embassy
35 rue du faubourg-Saint-Honoré
75008 Paris
tel: (010-33-1) 42-66-91-42

Consulate
9 av. Hoche
75008 Paris
tel: (010-33-1) 42-66-38-10
fax: (010-33-1) 40-76-02-87

British Consulate General
Bordeaux
353 blvd du Président-Wilson
33073 Bordeaux cédex
tel: (010-33) 56-42-34-13
fax: (010-33) 56-08-33-12

Lille
11 sq. Dutilleul
59800 Lille
tel: (010-33) 20-57-87-90
fax: (010-33) 20-54-88-16

Lyon
24 rue Childebert
69288 Lyon cédex
tel: (010-33) 78-37-59-67
fax: (010-33) 72-40-25-24

Marseille
24 av. du Prado
13006 Marseille
tel: (010-33) 91-53-43-32
fax: (010-33) 91-37-47-06

7 LETTING AND BED-AND-BREAKFAST

Many people hope to be able to make an income from their French home by letting it when they are not using it. If they are planning to buy in a country district, they may be thinking in terms of doing up an outbuilding for conversion into fairly basic self-catering accommodation, or for letting rooms on a bed-and-breakfast basis when they are there themselves.

The first thing to be said is that it takes time to build up to the stage where you will be able to make anything resembling a real income. Even then don't expect it to be substantial, except possibly in the mountains or in an expensive seaside resort. You will have to spend money equipping the place to the standards expected by holiday tenants. If you let through an agency, you'll have to pay quite high fees or commission. The season will be quite short in most areas of France. You will also have to declare any income for tax purposes.

You will also have to give a lot of thought to dealing with the problem of seeing tenants in and out. If you come to an agreement with a local agent or other service company to handle this, their fees will again eat into your income.

Bed-and-breakfast requires thought about advertising to catch passing trade and means that you must be very available.

French legislation

A distinction is made in law between year-round lets and holiday lets. Renting a home is very common in France and buying property to let out is more common than investing in stocks and shares, so a complex body of legislation exists both to protect tenants' rights and to ensure that it is worth landlords' while to let out their houses and flats.

Non-holiday lets

The basic principle underlying current legislation is that tenants have security of tenure for three years, but need give only three months' notice if they wish to leave, or one month if their departure becomes necessary for family reasons (like a death) or for work reasons (for instance if their firm moves them elsewhere or because they lose their job and have to move to find another one). The only exception might be if you decide you want to live there yourself and can give a good reason for needing to do so; but you'd still have to give at least six months' notice to your tenant.

You must therefore think very carefully before letting out your new flat or house and take legal advice on the letting contract. You will also need to check on the rent you can charge, the percentage of any service charges you can pass on to your tenants, and matters such as insurance – all of which are the subject of complex regulations.

The easiest way to find such tenants will be through a local agency. The FNAIM* (estate agents' federation) will be able to supply you with a list of agencies entitled to handle lettings. An advertisement in the national press in Britain might produce a long-term tenant if you want to let off a converted outbuilding or cottage that came with your purchase of a house in the country. You might, for instance, attract a writer or painter, with or without family, wanting a quiet place to work for a longish period.

Holiday lets
The majority of lets arranged by British owners of French holiday homes come under legislation governing holiday accommodation. This means furnished accommodation let for up to three months only, during the holiday season, to tenants whose permanent home is elsewhere, and who are not carrying on a business on your premises. The official holiday season varies from region to region: the summer months in the country or by the sea, winter in ski resorts, plus perhaps a brief summer season if the resort is also popular for walking and climbing. Provided you are letting in what is deemed to be a normal holiday area and the above criteria are met, there are no government controls. You are free to set your own rental charge and to let for whatever term suits you, without running the risk of not being able to get rid of your tenants. You will, of course, need to find out what type of rent is being charged in the area for similar accommodation, as market forces operate even when official controls don't.

Making the place lettable
The amount and quality of equipment and furnishings you put in for tenants will depend on the rent you hope to charge. There is a market both for very basic accommodation at low weekly or monthly rents and for much more luxurious accommodation at quite high rents. You must always bear in mind the sad truth that no one – not even friends – will care about the place as much as you do and be prepared to have to replace items broken or damaged. You should, of course, charge a deposit to cover such damage, but it is sensible not to leave any items to which you are particularly attached when you have tenants.

Think carefully about beds: double beds reduce the number of family permutations and therefore the potential market. Agents recommend having a cot available to attract families with babies. Folding beds and sofa beds are not popular with tenants.

You will need to provide enough cutlery and china and glasses for the number of people to whom you can let (generally counted as the number of sleeping places available, i.e. at least six sets of everything for a house with two double beds and two single, or twin beds and four single). But what you provide in the way of tableware and kitchenware will depend partly on whether you are letting to British or French tenants. For instance, if you plan to let mainly to British tenants they will appreciate a kettle, teapot, plenty of teacups, bowls for cereal, china mugs and egg cups. French tenants will be used to heating up water in a saucepan but will prefer bowls for morning coffee, small after-dinner size coffee cups for coffee at other times, a coffee pot, and soup plates rather than bowls. If in doubt about what to provide for French tenants, ask neighbours or any association through whom you plan to let (see below).

Pillows are another area for Franco-British comparisons. You will need to take account of this if you are expecting guests to bring their own bed linen. In France standard practice is to have a long bolster (called a *traversin*) and either no pillows at all or square pillows. But British guests will, of course, be bringing the standard rectangular pillow cases you are used to at home. If you expect your British guests to arrive by plane, they will not want to carry bed linen with them and will expect to find sheets, pillow cases and towels. In that case you must either charge for laundry or make arrangements for them to leave it at the local *blanchisserie* and pay for laundering before they leave.

Perhaps the biggest area of difference is that the French expect a large eating space – a room with a large dining table and plenty of chairs – but do not mind if there is no other sitting area. The British expect a living room with comfortable chairs for lounging but will be prepared to accept a kitchen-dining room.

The moral of all this is that it is easier to let either to British tenants or to French, rather than try to catch both markets.

If you are prepared to spend money putting in a swimming pool you will be able to command higher rents, but you will have to think who is to look after it when you aren't there: don't count on tenants doing the necessary checking of the pump and other maintenance.

Central heating, or electric convector radiators, will make it easier to ask a fairly high rent.

Finding tenants

Friends and friends of friends, work colleagues and their friends are an obvious source of potential tenants, with the advantage that you will not only either know them personally or have a reliable personal recommendation, but will be able to sort out various practical and logistical aspects at home – receiving the money, handing over keys and so on. If they like it so much that they come back year after year, or produce other friends to replace them, your letting problem is solved.

Realistically, it won't be quite as easy as that. If you want to find tenants for the full summer season plus Easter, a period of sixteen to twenty weeks, perhaps minus three to four weeks for yourselves, that still means quite a few different lets every year. And coordinating dates so that you don't finish up with a gap in the middle may be a problem.

A number of British agents specialise in letting French properties. And some estate agents handling French property sales offer a letting service for clients buying through them, and sometimes for those who have bought elsewhere. Such agencies advertise in the property sections of the national press and in specialist magazines. You must expect to pay a commission of at least 25 per cent simply for their finding tenants. They will provide you with lists of basic requirements and recommended extras for the type of tenants they supply – usually British – and advise you on rent.

The FNAIM* will be able to supply you with lists of local agents entitled to handle rented property, if the agent through whom you bought cannot help. Their tenants will mostly be French, with a sprinkling of foreigners of various nationalities. It may be helpful to know that the French are not on the whole interested in renting very comfortable (and therefore quite expensive) country places for their holidays, preferring seaside villas or mountain chalets, but they do go for modest rural accommodation. Local tourist offices in holiday areas often maintain a register of houses and flats available for rent, which vary widely from modest *gîte*-type accommodation to a wing of a château.

Joining the gîte association

The term *gîte* is now so widely known that it tends to be used loosely to describe any fairly modest rural dwelling let furnished to holiday-makers. But true *gîtes* are controlled by the Fédération nationale des gîtes ruraux,* who maintain minimum standards and publish booklets of property available by region, with a 'star' system (in fact ears of corn) to indicate facilities. *Gîtes* must normally be available for at least three months a year and can only be rented out when the owner is nearby. So this formula will be suitable only for converted outbuildings while you are staying in the main house, or conversely are letting out the main house while you are cosily ensconced in a separate cottage or outbuilding.

If your accommodation is approved by the federation you will be able to put up the familiar *gîte* sign and may benefit from certain tax advantages. However, you will normally be under an obligation to accept any potential tenants who have paid the membership fee. Check such aspects carefully before applying to become an official *gîte*.

Private advertising

Small ads in the British press are a traditional way of advertising self-catering accommodation in France. For instance, the property columns of the *Sunday Times*, the *Daily Telegraph* and the *Lady* all carry substantial numbers of such advertisements. If there is a successful regional daily in your part of the world, this may also be a good way of finding tenants, and simplifying the question of vetting them and handing over keys and instructions. If all goes well, they may recommend you to friends and you will have started to build up a pool of tenants.

It is sensible to ask for the rent in advance, in sterling, and to take a returnable deposit in case of breakages and other damage.

The tax position

Income tax is payable in France on income derived from letting property in France, even if the money is paid outside the country. (There are occasional exemptions if you are letting off a part of your main residence for a modest rent.) As a non-resident you should register with the Centre des Impôts des Non-résidents (9 rue d'Uzès, 75008 Paris) by 30 April, bearing in mind that there are penalties for non-registration as well as for being late with your tax return. If you are resident in Britain for income tax purposes, you must also declare any income received in France on your British tax return. Thanks to the double taxation treaty between France and the United Kingdom, tax paid in France is normally credited against any tax payable at home. But if you are hoping to let on a regular basis, it is wise to consult an expert on the tax implications in advance of your purchase, especially as the various laws and regulations change from time to time.

It may be possible to offset some of the initial costs of renovation and otherwise bringing up to letting standard, particularly if you are letting a separate outhouse converted specifically for the purpose. As a general rule the taxable income will be the rent minus local taxes, fees paid to an agent or other intermediary to let and manage the house or flat, and an allowance for depreciation and running costs. You may also be entitled to an allowance for interest on a bank loan or mortgage.

If you are going to be doing regular letting you may also have to charge your tenants VAT. Check with a financial and legal adviser. Ask their advice, too, when you first buy the property: if you are sure that you are going to be letting part of it out (perhaps an outhouse) it may be advisable to tell the *notaire* of this at the outset to ensure that you won't subsequently be bothered by the local bureaucracy. As a general rule in France, it is better to get the formalities sorted out in the first place, rather than risk paying a fine later because you have not complied.

If you are feeling overwhelmed by a deluge of paperwork connected with letting, look into the subscription service offered by estate agents Rutherfords.* Mainly used by owners of modern property, it is called the Rutherford's Administration Service and, in return for an annual fee (£110 in 1993), it handles all correspondence with the managing agents, developers, the local authority, gas and electricity boards and so on. Some legal firms with French property services may also be able to take this chore off your shoulders.

Prices

The price you can charge naturally depends on such factors as the attractiveness or otherwise of the region, and of the house or flat itself, and its accessibility, facilities and amenities. As a rough guideline, a modest *gîte*-type house with two bedrooms, a small living/dining room, small kitchen or kitchenette and shower room in a country district in the southwest could be let privately for 1,500–2,000 francs a week in 1993. A three-bedroomed house with heating and a good standard of comfort and modern conveniences in the same area would fetch 2,500–3,000 francs a week. A house big enough for two families, with a swimming pool, about 6,500–8,000 francs a week. All these are high summer prices, with mid-season (May, June and September) about 15 per cent lower and low season about 45 per cent lower. They do not include an agent's commission. Villas on the Côte d'Azur naturally command much higher rents.

Managing the lets

Unless you are prepared to rush over to France every time a tenant arrives or leaves, you will have to come to some arrangement with a local agent or other intermediary. Such a service will involve: handing over and taking in keys; checking that the detailed inventory you have prepared is still accurate; dealing with any dramas that may occur (power failures, break-ins, problems with swimming pools); and generally keeping an eye on tenants. A number of British firms have set up management services of this kind, including taking care of any running repairs needed, informing owners of any breakages and buying replacements with their authorisation. A typical charge is £30–35 a week. Ask around locally, or look for advertisements in the British specialist press.

Points to remember

As well as preparing an inventory and making sure that nothing particularly fragile or precious is left in the house or flat, there are various things you must remember to tell your tenants about. If you are letting a flat in a condominium it is essential that you should show them the *règlement de copropriété* (Chapter 1) and impress on them any key regulations, such as use of swimming pool or not disturbing neighbours after 10 p.m. In the country, remember that British tenants probably won't be familiar with *fosses septiques*, so you must leave large notices all over the place warning them about not putting any foreign bodies down the lavatory and only using suitable cleaning products. French tenants may be more familiar with such matters, but don't count on it.

Your tenants are more likely to come back again and again if you provide them with friendly hints about local shops, restaurants, beauty spots, museums and so on. A loose-leaf folder to which you can add information as appropriate is the best way of doing this. Encourage them to add their own tips for other tenants.

You should tell your insurance company that you are letting. Otherwise if there is a break-in you may find that you are not covered.

Bed-and-breakfast

The French have now taken to the idea of B-&-B and *chambres d'hôtes* (guest rooms) are widely used by French holidaymakers as well as other nationalities. You do not need a special licence to provide B-&-B, but you must register with the local trade registry (*registre du commerce*) within two weeks of starting your B-&-B business. You are generally limited to six rooms before being classified as a full-scale guest house or hotel. If you intend to provide some meals other than breakfast, you will need a permit to serve wine; ask at the *mairie*.

As with the letting of outbuildings, it is advisable to make it clear to the *notaire* and any separate legal adviser if you are planning to let more than six rooms, as you will have to pay higher duties on the transaction and could be subject to penalties and interest if the situation emerges at some subsequent date. If you buy a building or buildings previously run as a B-&-B, and decide to purchase the furniture and other equipment, the legal fees will be higher still.

Finding customers

You can apply to the *gîtes* federation* and if you are accepted will be able to display the familiar *chambre d'hôte* board with its logo of a bed and steaming cup of coffee beneath a roof with smoking chimney. Another association whose members offer the B-&-B formula is the equally alliterative Café Couette* (meaning coffee-and-duvet). Some local Chambres d'agriculture* run farm holiday schemes, usually called 'Bienvenue à la ferme', and in areas popular with tourists, the local *syndicat d'initiative* or *office de tourisme* (tourist office) may maintain a card index of people willing to offer B-&-B – you could apply to be included.

If you particularly want British customers you could try advertising in the specialist press.

Rosemary and Peter Farley, running a château and farm in the Touraine with five *chambres d'hôte*, stressed the importance of being visible from the road: if your house is tucked away down a distant path you will lose many potential customers. If necessary, you will have to put up a board some way away directing people to your house. If it is to go on someone else's land you will obviously need that person's permission. The local office of the Direction départementale d'équipement (known as the DDE) authorises signs beside roads and will probably have strict regulations about sizes and heights. Check before you commission your sign or paint one yourself.

Keeping customers happy

Rosemary Farley insisted that you must be not only very available but also a mine of authoritative information about the tourist sights for miles around, and on leisure facilities, as well as on doctors, the nearest chemist and local shops. You must also speak quite good French. It would help if you can get by in another language too.

The Farleys suggested keeping a scrapbook of local information, picking up a pile of brochures and leaflets at the beginning of each tourist season on the museums, châteaux, nature reserves and the like in the region, and putting a folder containing all these in each room, plus cards garnered from local restaurants. You must, they added, like people!

Useful addresses

Café Couette
8 rue d'Isly
75008 Paris
tel: (010-33-1) 42-94-92-00

Fédération nationale des Gîtes de France
35 rue Godot-de-Mauroy
75439 Paris cédex 09
tel: (010-33-1) 47-42-20-20
The association has many regional branches; write with international reply coupon for the address of your nearest branch.

Assemblée permanente des Chambres d'agriculture
9 av. George-V
75008 Paris
tel: (010-33-1) 47-23-55-40
Write with international reply coupon for address of local chamber and details of *Bienvenue à la ferme* scheme.

Some British agents letting property in France

Bowhills
Mayhill Farm
Swanmore SO3 2QW
tel: Bishop's Waltham
(0489) 877 627
fax: Bishop's Waltham
(0489) 877 872
Covers the whole of western and south-western France, plus the centre (Loire, Auvergne) and Provence and the Côte d'Azur.

Eurovillas
36 East Street
Coggeshall
Essex CO6 1SH
tel: Coggeshall (0376) 561 156
Brittany, Dordogne, Tarn, Roussillon, south-east.

Pieds à terre
Barker Chambers
Barker Road
Maidstone
Kent ME16 8SF
tel: Maidstone (0622) 688 165
fax: Maidstone (0622) 671 840

Francophiles estate agency's letting service specialises in Brittany, Normandy, Pas de Calais, Dordogne and the Vendée. Interested in hearing from people with comfortable places to let (not basic *gîte*-type accommodation), especially near sea or with pool.

French Country Holidays
Anglia House
Marina
Lowestoft
Suffolk NR32 1PZ
tel: Lowestoft (0502) 517 271
fax: Lowestoft (0502) 500 970
West and central France, plus Provence and the Alps.

French Villas
175 Selsdon Park Road
South Croydon
Surrey CR2 8JJ
tel: 081-651 1231
fax: 081-651 4920
Seaside villas in Normandy, Brittany, south-west and south.

Premier France
The Courtyard
Arlington Road
Surbiton
Surrey KT6 6BW
tel: 081-390 3335
fax: 081-390 6378

A subsidiary of Crystal Holidays, specialising in villas, cottages and châteaux in Brittany, the Dordogne, on the Côte d'Azur and the Atlantic Coast.

8   SELLING YOUR HOME

Some articles in the British press have suggested that large numbers of British people hit by the recession have had to put their French homes on the market. The picture has undoubtedly been exaggerated, and according to banks and agents the majority of the sellers belong to the category of unrealistic optimists who moved to France without looking properly into the level of income they could expect to earn, or who did not make allowances for factors such as a drop in sterling's value against the franc. However some second-home owners have also been forced into selling, and anyway, you may simply want to move to a different part of France.

Much of the information you need to know about selling property in France is already included in Chapter 3 – except that you are bound to look at things slightly differently when you're the seller rather than the buyer. Never forget either that legislation and local practice do change from time to time, so don't automatically assume that the sale will proceed in exactly the same way as when you bought.

Finding a buyer

The one thing you can't normally do is have a board put up. 'For sale' boards are rarely used in France, though they have become a more common sight as people try to mitigate the effects of the recession by selling privately. However they may still be prohibited under local bye-laws.

If you are in an area where the seller pays the commission you may think it worth trying to go it alone without an agent. The easiest method may be to try to find a buyer through friends in Britain or in France, or through the local expatriate community if there is one. Here you can take advantage of French agents' frequent reluctance to produce detailed particulars to attract buyers. When an agent failed to find me a buyer for a house at what she said was the right price, I sold it quite quickly myself by typing out a very detailed description covering two A4 sheets. It included exact measurements of each room, number of radiators, even the plants in the garden. I made fifty photocopies and handed them out to neighbours and shopkeepers, the doctor and the local school. A buyer soon materialised – a friend of a neighbour – and in no time at all we were signing a *promesse de vente* in the *notaire*'s office.

If yours is the type of place likely to appeal to British buyers, you could try putting a card in the window of a shop frequented by the local British community, or, if there is such a thing, on the noticeboard of a church or club frequented by British residents.

Otherwise you can try one of the newspapers or magazines referred to in Chapter 4. But bear in mind that advertising in the British national press is expensive and won't necessarily produce results. The specialist press will work out considerably cheaper, as well as ensuring that you reach your target market.

If you do find a British purchaser, there is nothing to prevent you receiving the purchase price in sterling in Britain, though normal practice is for the money to be paid via a solicitor, not direct to you. The buyer will still have to pay the legal fees in francs direct to the *notaire*. Do make sure, if you take this route, that you will have enough funds in France to be able to settle all outstanding bills and pay for removal costs and the like. Experts advise that this type of sale is not recommended if either you or your buyer is resident in France for tax purposes.

In a difficult market, you might like to consider a deal whereby some of the sale price is paid at a later date. You could also look into the possibility of exchanging your French home for somewhere in Britain.

If you are not buying a new French home, you should consider including your furniture in the sale price. This might well be an attractive proposition for, say, another British family, as it would save them a great deal of time and trouble. And second-hand furniture and household appliances usually command even lower prices in France than in Britain, so it would scarcely be worth your while going through the hassle of selling them separately.

I must refer once again to the severe penalties incurred by those who are caught taking some of the purchase price 'under the table' to avoid capital gains tax, or to fall in with a buyer's attempt to reduce the taxes and fees payable on the transaction. Stephen Smith of Prettys* stresses that such transactions are strictly illegal: there are serious criminal sanctions against those perpetrating what is deemed to be a fraud, and against their accomplices, and they also incur civil and criminal penalties. You have been warned!

Using an agent

Giving an exclusive agency is not as common as in Britain, but you could try doing so for a limited period if you think it will spur him/her on. If you do so, this will be included in the *mandat* authorising the agent to act for you.

Check carefully any preliminary contract produced by the agent, preferably having it vetted by an independent legal adviser. Once again, it is wiser to insist on a preliminary agreement signed at a *notaire*'s office. If you were happy with the service provided by the *notaire* when you bought the house or flat, and he is still in business, the simplest way is to use him again, as he will have all the details of the sale to you on file. Otherwise you will have to dig out the copy of the deed of sale and show it to the agent and any other *notaire* you use. Remember that the buyer is entitled to bring in a second *notaire*. If you're selling a flat, you'll also have to dig out the *règlement de copropriété*, and be prepared to give details of any work that is due to be carried out (this will be checked by the *notaire* with the *syndic* of the block or development).

Capital gains tax (CGT)

This is the bad news when you go to sell a holiday home in France: you will be liable for capital gains tax in France, unless you have owned the place for thirty-two years or longer (not twenty-two years as was the case until a short while ago). But thanks to the double-taxation treaty you will not have to pay in Britain as well, as any tax you pay in France will be set against any CGT liability at home.

Calculating whether there has been a capital gain involves deducting the purchase price plus either 10 per cent (a flat rate representing the various fees and costs you had to pay at the time of your purchase) or the actual legal costs, if this is more favourable to you, from the proceeds you will receive from the sale (less agent's commission, where relevant, if it is payable by the vendor in your part of France). You can also deduct any renovation and restoration costs, provided you have kept proper receipts from the various builders and craftsmen and for materials; these receipts must include VAT. Ordinary painting and decorating won't count though. Fees charged by a tax adviser can also be deducted, and so can interest payments on a mortgage in some circumstances. Various other allowances may be permissible and there is also an official indexation allowance based on the rate of inflation between the dates of purchase and sale. The longer you have owned the property the lower your capital gains tax liability and it dwindles to nothing once you reach the thirty-two years.

Don't sell in less than two years if you can possibly avoid it, as in that case you cannot claim any of the special allowances. The only exception to this would be if you had to sell for a pressing family reason such as a death or possibly for work reasons (for instance if you were posted to the United States or Africa and therefore could no longer use your French home).

If you have meanwhile moved to France, so that your holiday home has become your permanent residence, no capital gains tax will normally be payable after five years of permanent residence for at least eight months of each year.

CGT is also normally not payable on a first sale of a second home by a non-resident who has been tax-domiciled in France and filed a tax return for at least one year at some point in the past, provided that the house or flat has not been let, and the vendor has had free disposal of it for either a minimum of five years, or since it was bought or built.

The rate of capital gains tax is 33⅓ per cent. Don't make a habit of buying and selling. The French are not great ones for doing up places and then moving on. If you do so, the tax authorities will suspect that you are really a dealer in property and may charge you 50 per cent.

Appointing a guarantor

If you sell as a non-resident, whether or not there is a capital gains tax liability, you won't get the proceeds of the sale until you have appointed a guarantor to be responsible for any further tax claimed by the tax authorities during the rest of the year after the sale and the following three years. (During that period they are entitled to re-examine the calculation and come back to you with a further claim.) The guarantor can be a bank or a private individual resident in France for tax purposes, or an organisation specialising in this matter. It can also be the purchaser, as long as he or she is a French taxpayer. But as there is no upper limit to the guarantee, your purchaser is likely to be understandably wary of agreeing to this – and if French, will be puzzled by this regulation, applicable only to non-residents. Unfortunately banks and other approved institutions make substantial charges for this service.

However, you may be able to get a dispensation from this rule if there is clearly no capital gains tax liability, or if the calculation is so straightforward that there is no likelihood whatsoever of there ever being a further tax demand. It is worth taking this up with the *notaire* well before completion date. If you are using a separate legal adviser he/she should be able to help here. Caroline Jenkins of Office notarial de Fréjus* also warns that this dispensation will take four to six weeks to come through.

VAT liability

If you are selling a house or flat built within the last five years, of which you were the first owner, there may be a liability to pay TVA – check this with the *notaire* and/or legal adviser.

Receiving the proceeds

In most cases the proceeds will not be handed over to you on the day the *acte authentique* is signed, particularly if you had a mortgage on the house or flat. But they might be (see Chapter 3) and it is a good idea to ask the *notaire* about this, so that you know where you stand.

If you are having to pay capital gains tax this will be deducted from the proceeds. So will the agent's commission if the seller pays in that part of France.

Dealing with utilities and services

It is up to you to read meters with the buyer and work out who owes what for water and so on when the next bill comes in. Don't forget to send a registered letter with advice of delivery slip to your insurance company to cancel your policy or you'll find that it is renewed automatically and you'll be liable for the premium. The company may also ask for a copy of the deed of sale, and may refuse to cancel your policy until the buyer has confirmed that he/she will be insuring the place from the day of the sale.

If you have bought somewhere else in France, transferring your electricity contract and your telephone contract to your new home will be quite straightforward and you may even be able to do it on the telephone nowadays, provided your French is good enough. Otherwise allow quite some time to persuade the bureaucrats who inhabit the various offices that you really are leaving and you'll have a lot of letters and forms to deal with.

Selling at auction

Selling property at auction is quite common in France, particularly after a death when the heirs want to sell up. Auctions are run by *notaires*, who value the property and offer guidance on the starting price and fixing a reserve price.

Private auctions, which may be the result not only of a death, but of a dispute between joint owners, or arise because someone in difficulties with mortgage repayments expects to get a better price before the lender insists on repossession, are advertised locally in the local press and by bill posting.

Those who wish to bid must produce 20 per cent of the floor price before the auction starts; non-residents may have to pay more – 40 per cent in some cases. If you are an unsuccessful bidder your money of course will be returned. In the country you may be able to bid in person; in towns you will have to appoint someone from a *notaire*'s office to bid for you. Either way it is quite a dramatic business. The auctioneer starts off by lighting a candle. This will stay alight throughout the auction. When the bidding stops he must light another, smaller candle, which burns for only about twenty seconds. If there are no more bids before it goes out, he will light another quick-burning candle. When that has gone out the property goes to the person who bid the highest figure, and the other bidders are reimbursed.

However, further written bids can be made during the ten days following the auction, though they must be at least 10 per cent higher than the winning bid. If no more bids come in, the deal is made.

Legal costs are high on auctions: about double that for an ordinary sale. And there are no let-out clauses concerning the obtaining of a loan, so bidders in need of a loan must get that agreed in advance.

In the case of repossession or bankruptcy, the auction is conducted by the courts and the process is slightly different.

INDEX